CONCISE GUIDE TO
Brief Dynamic Psychotherapy

American Psychiatric Press

CONCISE GUIDES

Robert E. Hales, M.D.
Series Editor

CONCISE GUIDE TO
Brief Dynamic Psychotherapy

Hanna Levenson, Ph.D.
Stephen F. Butler, Ph.D.
Bernard D. Beitman, M.D.

Washington, DC
London, England

Copyright © 1997 American Psychiatric Press, Inc.
ALL RIGHTS RESERVED
Manufactured in the United States of America on acid-free paper
First Edition
00 99 98 97   4   3   2   1
American Psychiatric Press, Inc.
1400 K Street, N.W., Washington, DC   20005
www.appi.org

Library of Congress Cataloging-in-Publication Data
Levenson, Hanna, 1945–
    Concise guide to brief dynamic psychotherapy / Hanna Levenson,
Stephen F. Butler, Bernard D. Beitman. — 1st ed.
        p.   cm. — (Concise guides / American Psychiatric Press)
    Includes bibliographical references and index.
    ISBN 0-88048-346-6 (alk. paper)
    1. Psychodynamic psychotherapy.   2. Brief psychotherapy.
I. Butler, Stephen F., 1950–   . II. Beitman, Bernard D.
III. Series: Concise guides (American Psychiatric Press)
    [DNLM: 1. Psychotherapy, Brief—methods.   WM 420.5.P5
    L657c 1997]
RC489.P72L48   1997
616.89′14—dc21
DNLM/DLC
for Library of Congress   97-17250
                                                                                    CIP

British Library Cataloguing in Publication Data
A CIP record is available from the British Library.

CONTENTS

7. BRIEF DYNAMIC PSYCHOTHERAPY FOR PATIENTS WITH SUBSTANCE ABUSE DISORDERS 123

8. BRIEF PSYCHODYNAMIC PSYCHOTHERAPY WITH CHILDREN 149

9. THE RECIPROCAL RELATIONSHIP BETWEEN PHARMACOTHERAPY AND PSYCHOTHERAPY 173

ABOUT THE AUTHORS

Hanna Levenson, Ph.D., is Director of the Brief Psychotherapy Programs at the Veterans Administration Medical Center and the California Pacific Medical Center and Founder of the Levenson Institute for Training (LIFT) in Brief Therapy in San Francisco, California. She is Clinical Professor in the Department of Psychiatry at the University of California School of Medicine in San Francisco and maintains a private practice in San Francisco and Oakland, California.

Stephen F. Butler, Ph.D., is Vice President of Innovative Training Systems, Inc., a research and consulting firm based in Massachusetts. Prior to this position, he held faculty appointments in the Vanderbilt Psychology Department and the Psychiatry Department of the Medical College of Virginia. He was also Director of Psychology at Nashua Brookside Hospital, Nashua, New Hampshire.

Bernard D. Beitman, M.D., is Professor and Chairman in the Department of Psychiatry and Neurology at the University of Missouri-Columbia School of Medicine.

INTRODUCTION

to the American Psychiatric Press Concise Guides

The American Psychiatric Press *Concise Guides* series provides practical information for psychiatrists, psychiatry residents, and medical students working in a variety of treatment settings, such as inpatient psychiatry units, outpatient clinics, consultation-liaison services, or private office settings. The *Concise Guides* are meant to complement the more detailed information to be found in lengthier psychiatry texts.

The *Concise Guides* address topics of special concern to psychiatrists in clinical practice. The books in this series contain a detailed table of contents, along with an index, tables, figures, and other charts for easy access. The books are designed to fit into a lab coat pocket or jacket pocket, which makes them a convenient source of information. The number of references has been limited to those most relevant to the material presented.

The authors of the *Concise Guide to Brief Dynamic Psychotherapy* are experienced clinicians as well as academicians in the field of brief psychotherapy. Dr. Levenson has directed the brief psychotherapy programs at the University of California, San Francisco Veterans Administration Medical Center, and at the California Pacific Medical Center's Department of Psychiatry for a number of years. Dr. Butler has been a member of the faculties of the Departments of Psychology and Psychiatry at Vanderbilt and the Medical College of Virginia. Lastly, Dr. Beitman is Professor and Chairman in the Department of Psychiatry and Neurology at the University of Missouri-Columbia School of Medicine.

The authors begin their book by discussing those qualities that define brief dynamic therapy and outline values and attitudes that are important for the clinician to keep in mind when using this therapeutic modality. Drs. Levenson, Butler, and Beitman have included an excellent chapter on supportive psychotherapy. It is difficult to find well-written articles on this important type of brief therapy. Readers will note that each chapter includes a section on the relevance of the particular therapeutic approach to managed care. The authors discuss, in addition to supportive therapy, time-limited therapy, interpersonal psychotherapy for depression, time-limited dynamic psychotherapy, and short-term dynamic therapy for posttraumatic stress disorders, substance abuse disorders, and childhood disorders. A particularly important chapter is titled, "The Reciprocal Relationship Between Pharmacotherapy and Psycho-therapy." As many clinicians know, in today's managed care era, often the psychiatric treatment of patients is divided between a pharmacotherapist and a psychotherapist. The authors provide practical guidelines for clinicians to consider when this combined approach is required.

This excellent book includes a wealth of information of inter-est to practicing psychiatrists, psychologists, and social workers and trainees in each of these fields. The authors have included a number of outstanding tables that summarize important informa-tion presented in the text. Readers should be pleased with the clear and precise prose and the book's clinical relevance. The material contained in this book, including the references, is quite current and of the highest quality, and the authors have thoroughly and carefully reviewed the current literature. They address many con-troversies in the field of brief psychotherapy and provide a sound basis for their treatment recommendations.

The *Concise Guide to Brief Dynamic Psychotherapy* is a beautifully written, pocket-sized book that should be of invaluable assistance to psychiatrists and other mental health professionals. Also, residents and other trainees should find it an excellent addi-tion to their professional library.

Robert E. Hales, M.D.
Series Editor
American Psychiatric Press Concise Guides

INTRODUCTION

■ FOCUS OF THE BOOK

Psychodynamic Orientation

In writing this book, we have taken the position that the clinician who is trying to institute time-limited or time-efficient approaches needs to operate from a systematic, theoretically based model. As Kurt Lewin, a social psychologist, is credited with stating, "There is nothing so practical as a good theory" (1, p. viii). We have chosen to focus on psychodynamically based or dynamically informed models, but not because psychodynamic theory is the be-all and end-all of all approaches. In fact, there is now ample empirical evidence that most "schools" of therapy achieve approximately the same magnitude of outcomes, and all do better than no treatment or various types of control groups (2).

We have instead selected various psychodynamic treatment models to present here because

> dynamic psychiatry simply provides a coherent conceptual framework within which all treatments are prescribed. Regardless of whether the treatment is dynamic psychotherapy or pharmacotherapy, it is dynamically informed. (3, p. 4)

Portions of this chapter were reprinted from Levenson H, Hales RE: "Brief Psychodynamically Informed Therapy for Medically Ill Patients," in *Medical-Psychiatric Practice,* Vol 2. Edited by Stoudemire A, Fogel BS. Washington, DC, American Psychiatric Press, 1993, pp. 3–37. Copyright © 1993, American Psychiatric Press. Used with permission.

This viewpoint is supported by the conclusion of the joint task force of the Association for Academic Psychiatry and the American Association of Directors of Psychiatry Residency Training (4), which held that psychodynamic psychotherapy is critical in general psychiatry education.

In short, a deep, usable understanding of and ability to apply clinically the concepts of a dynamic unconscious, transference and countertransference, and mental defense mechanisms are central to being an effective pharmacotherapist, behavior therapist, inpatient psychiatrist, consultation psychiatrist, and, perhaps, even a laboratory research psychiatrist (p. 9).

As Perry et al. (5), writing on the topic of psychodynamic formulation, stated,

> Therapeutic effectiveness or failure often hinges on how well or poorly the therapist understands the patient's dynamics, predicts what resistances the patient will present, and designs an approach that will circumvent, undermine, or surmount these obstacles. (p. 543)

A recent national random survey of 4,000 mental health professionals (6) found that one-half of psychiatrists and one-quarter of psychologists and social workers identified themselves as having a purely psychodynamic orientation. An additional 40% overall held an eclectic or integrative stance. Thus the psychodynamic perspective has been and remains quite robust and fundamental to the day-to-day practice of clinicians.

Throughout this book we define *psychodynamically informed therapies* as those that consider, to a greater or lesser degree, the importance of early development, unconscious determinants of behavior, conflict, the therapeutic relationship between therapist and patient (including transference and countertransference), patients' resistance to the work, and repetitive behavior. We do not, however, present psychodynamic models that use complex, highly inferential constructs (e.g., oral, anal, and phallic stages of development) and require adoption of an elaborate, metapsychological framework with unclear behavioral referents (e.g., id, ego, and superego). Rather, we have selected dynamic approaches that adhere closely to the observable data, because they have been shown to be quite clinically useful and didactically teachable.

Brief Psychotherapy

To the novice reader it may seem that brief psychotherapy is a recent phenomenon brought on by the advent of managed care and third-party payers as a result of the shrinking mental health dollar. However, for years patients themselves have been electing to be treated "briefly" by choosing to stay in therapy for an average of six to eight sessions, regardless of the type of outpatient treatment they are receiving (7, 8). These findings hold even for treatments that are intended to be long term (9). It has been estimated that 90% of all patients leave treatment by the 10th session. Although we do not know precisely the reasons for these dropouts, improvement data indicate that approximately 50% of patients report considerable benefit by the eighth session (10).

Most patients who present for therapy are in emotional pain. They want to have their pain alleviated as soon as possible. Most of them are not fascinated by their psyches, nor are they pursuing mental health perfection.

These consumer-defined brief therapies, or what have been called *naturally occurring brief therapies,* are quite different from therapies that are planned from the start to make the most of limited time. Brief therapies by default, which has been the norm, are in contrast to the therapies presented here, which are brief therapies by design.

Outcome data for planned short-term therapies indicate that the average patient receiving brief therapy does better than 80% of untreated control subjects (11). In fact, empirical studies have failed to demonstrate that long-term approaches achieve better measurable outcomes than short-term therapies:

> Since brief therapy requires less time (for both therapist and patient) and therefore less social cost, it has been suggested that brief methods are equally effective and more cost efficient than long-term psychotherapy. (11, p. 692)

Today, because of limited mental health resources, emphasis on accountability, the concerns of third-party payers, and consumer need, there is an increasing demand for mental health professionals to use briefer therapeutic approaches. In the Davidovitz and Levenson national practitioner survey (6), 84% of all clinicians said they are doing some form of planned brief therapy for a portion of their practices.

Brief Dynamic Approaches

Traditionally, 25 sessions has been defined as marking the upper limit of brief dynamic therapies (11), but in practice, the range may be a few as 1 (12) or as many as 40 (13). Although many health maintenance organizations have a stated limit of 20 sessions per year, usually for crisis intervention or medical necessity, their average is closer to 6 sessions. Other settings impose various time limits, but most fall between 6 and 20 visits.

Recently, however, there has been a movement away from considering brief therapy merely in terms of the number of sessions. Instead, researchers, theoreticians, and clinicians are talking about time-attentive models that try to make every session count, regardless of the length of treatment. Here the emphasis is on the therapist's and the patient's time-limited attitude, and terms such as *time-effective*, *time-sensitive*, and *cost-effective* seem more relevant.

As expected in the nationwide practitioner survey (6), psychodynamically oriented therapists reported that they spent fewer hours in brief therapy than did their colleagues with other theoretical orientations. Because the dynamic therapists comprised such a large proportion of the sample, however, they were responsible for one-fourth of all the brief therapy being conducted in the United States. Unfortunately, the survey data also indicate that the psychodynamic practitioners who were doing brief therapy had received significantly less training in it, felt less skilled to do it, and judged it to be less effective than did their colleagues trained in other orientations.

These findings are alarming from a consumer perspective. It is now widely accepted that brief therapy is not dehydrated long-term therapy (14) nor just less of the same (15), but rather requires specialized training in its own methodology (16, 17). Therapists who are trained in brief therapy and follow specified methods have better outcomes than those who do not (18- 20), and trained clinicians feel that they are better skilled in brief therapy than are their untrained counterparts (21). Yet it seems apparent that a major discrepancy exists between the demand and the supply of professionals who are prepared to use time-efficient methods effectively. This *Concise Guide* on individual, brief dynamic therapies is a step in the direction of helping to educate both beginning and experienced clinicians in the strategies and techniques of brief dynamic therapeutic models.

■ QUALITIES THAT DEFINE BRIEF DYNAMIC THERAPY

In a content analysis of books and articles addressing essential features that distinguish brief dynamic from long-term dynamic therapy, Levenson and Butler (17) found a number of fundamental qualities pertinent to brief therapy that were repeatedly mentioned. Table 1–1 contains a list of these qualities, rank ordered in terms of the frequency with which they are mentioned in the literature. This list provides a consensual, operational definition of short-term dynamic psychotherapy. All of the therapies presented in this book manifest these characteristics to some extent.

TABLE 1–1.	Qualities that define brief dynamic psychotherapy

Limited focus and limited goals

Time limits and time management

Specific selection criteria

Therapist activity

Need to develop a therapeutic alliance quickly

Rapid assessment

Termination

Optimism on the part of the therapist

Treatment contract

Source. Adapted from Levenson H, Butler SF: "Brief Dynamic Individual Psychotherapy," in *The American Psychiatric Press Textbook of Psychiatry,* 2nd Edition. Edited by Hales RE, Yudofsky SC, Talbott JA. Washington, DC, American Psychiatric Press, 1994, p. 1012. Copyright © 1994, American Psychiatric Press. Used with permission.

■ VALUES AND ATTITUDES

Unfortunately, it is not just for lack of didactic information that there are not more psychodynamically oriented therapists who feel more skilled in applying brief interventions. Because many dynamic clinicians operate from an orientation that has valued long-term, depth-oriented work, they have resistances toward learning short-term methods, despite clinical advances and outcome data that demonstrate their effectiveness. Such clinicians may hold a number of myths or erroneous beliefs that make them reluctant to learn briefer interventions. Table 1–2 lists some sources of resistance toward briefer therapies and can be reviewed in order to assess one's own resistance level.

Budman and Gurman (22) proposed that the value system of the long-term therapist is significantly different from that of the short-term therapist. They suggested that one of the critical criteria for defining the nature of brief therapy is "a state of mind of the therapist and of the patient" (22, p. 278), rather than the number of sessions or the length of treatment. These authors postulated eight

TABLE 1–2.   **Sources of resistance against short-term dynamic psychotherapy**

1. The belief that "more is better"

2. Therapeutic "perfectionism"

3. Confusion of patient's interests with therapist's interests

4. Demands of greater activity and intense alertness

5. May be less profitable and dependable

6. Therapist's conflicts around separation and loss

7. Therapist's conflicts around attachment with new patients

8. Therapist's negative reaction to being told what to do

9. The need to be needed

10. Insecurities regarding one's own skill

11. Anxiety over the loss of one's professional role

12. Overconcern for "successful" termination

Source.   Adapted from Bauer GP, Kobos JC: *Brief Therapy: Short-Term Psychodynamic Intervention.* Northvale, NJ, Jason Aronson, 1987; Hoyt MF: "Therapist Resistances to Short-Term Dynamic Psychotherapy." *Journal of the American Academy of Psychoanalysis* 13:93–112, 1985; and Martin ES, Schurtman R: "Termination Anxiety as It Affects the Therapist." *Psychotherapy* 22:92–96, 1985.

dominant values pertaining to the ideal manner in which long-term therapy is practiced. They then contrasted these values with the corresponding ideal values that are pertinent to the practice of short-term therapy. Table 1–3 lists the comparative dominant values of the long-term and the short-term therapist.

In an empirical study, Bolter et al. (23) found that for two of the eight dominant values, responses were different between therapists who prefer doing long-term therapy and those who prefer short-term approaches. Specifically, short-term therapists believed more strongly that psychological change occurs after therapy (value 4) and that setting time limits intensifies the therapeutic work (value 5). However, the results also indicated that clinicians with a psy-

---

TABLE 1–3. **Comparative dominant values of the long-term and the short-term therapist**

Long-term therapist	Short-term therapist
1. Change in basic character	Least radical intervention, does not believe in the notion of "cure."
2. Significant psychological change is unlikely in everyday life.	Adult developmental perspective; psychological change is inevitable.
3. Presenting problems reflect more basic pathology.	Presenting problems are taken seriously (although not always at face value).
4. "Be there" as patient makes significant changes.	Many changes will occur "after therapy."
5. Therapy has a "timeless" quality; therapist is patient.	Therapy is finite; therapist is active.
6. Fiscal convenience of maintaining long-term patients.	Fiscal issues are muted by an organizational structure.
7. Psychotherapy is almost always benign and useful.	Psychotherapy is sometimes useful, sometimes harmful.
8. Therapy is the most important part of the patient's life.	Being in the world is more important than being in therapy.

Source. Reprinted from Budman SH, Gurman AS: *Theory and Practice of Brief Psychotherapy.* New York, Guilford, 1988, p. 11. Copyright © 1988, The Guilford Press. Used with permission.

---

chodynamic orientation (in contrast to those trained in cognitive-behavioral models) were more likely to believe that therapy is necessary for change (value 2), that therapy should be open-ended (value 5), and that ambitious goals are desirable (value 1). Thus, these findings suggest that although one's preferred approach (short- versus long-term) is related to therapeutic values, the therapist's theoretical orientation (psychodynamic versus cognitive-behavioral) also plays a significant role.

In the national practitioner survey (6), 90% of psychodynamic therapists said they preferred doing long-term and moderately long-term therapy. Thus, we can expect that a sizable number of therapists are in conflict—doing brief work they do not believe in, feel skilled in, or prefer to do, but out of economic or administrative constraints feel pressured to do. Without proper training and positive attitudes, we can expect poorer therapeutic outcomes done by professionals who feel "burned out" and demoralized.

We therefore hope that this *Concise Guide* will not only help educate clinicians that brief psychodynamic approaches have much to offer in the meaningful treatment of people presenting for help but also foster more positive and optimistic attitudes toward using brief therapy.

■ SPECIFIC MODELS PRESENTED

Eight psychodynamic brief individual therapy models are presented in this volume:

1. Supportive therapy
2. Time-limited therapy
3. Interpersonal therapy
4. Time-limited dynamic psychotherapy
5. Short-term dynamic therapy for posttraumatic stress disorder
6. Brief dynamic therapy for substance abuse disorders
7. Brief psychodynamic psychotherapy with children
8. Pharmacotherapy and psychotherapy integration

These eight models were chosen because they represent well-established, short-term approaches to clinical issues that therapists commonly encounter in their clinical practices. In addition, most of them have clearly defined intervention techniques and formulation strategies that should help the novice as well as the experienced clinician who wishes to use brief interventions in a more informed manner. We also tried to select models that could be used within the 10- to 20-session time frame of most managed care settings. Nonetheless, many of these approaches are equally applicable regardless of the length of the treatment. (One notable exception is that of James Mann, discussed in Chapter 3.)

The above list is not meant to be exhaustive or representative. We do think, however, that the psychodynamically informed practitioner who is knowledgeable about these eight models has an enormous armamentarium of clinical interventions to help patients in a time-efficient and effective manner.

In each chapter, a different model is discussed in terms of its overall framework, selection criteria, goals, therapeutic tasks and strategies, empirical support, and relevance for managed care. Clinical cases are used to illustrate the application of each model. In addition, a chapter on the use of psychopharmacotherapy is provided from the standpoint of the dynamically informed use of medications.

In addition, at the beginning of each chapter are listed the various presenting problems we think are most suitable for treatment by that particular approach. Although psychodynamic models have often been used generically to treat all individuals for every problem, we are impressed with how each model seems more applicable to certain types of problems and/or particular patients. By highlighting these relevant problems, we hope the practitioner will be guided to consider using a particular approach for reasons other than previous indoctrination, bias, or lack of knowledge.

Some problems are so prominent or overwhelming that the clinician should first consider using a treatment specifically designed to treat them. For example, for significant substance abuse, one should use models designed to treat that problem before considering treatment for other (presumably less pressing) problems. The sophisticated and experienced clinician will be able to combine aspects from various approaches to treat more precisely any combination of presenting problems. Because all of these approaches are basically psychodynamic in orientation, they can maintain an overall coherence if several are blended. The eight treatment models can be characterized by the degree to which they use supportive versus expressive techniques, focus on acute versus chronic problems, target changes in symptoms versus personality, and highlight intrapsychic versus interpersonal dynamics.

Because this a concise guide, the reader is given just a brief overview to each approach. We hope that the clinical and empirical relevance of these models will whet the reader's appetite to delve further into learning more about them. In each chapter we identify the major references for additional reading. Of course, no one can learn therapy—brief, dynamic, or otherwise—solely from books. We therefore encourage readers to also obtain clinical supervision in the particular approaches in order to practice them with sophistication and satisfaction.

■ REFERENCES

1. Marrow AJ: The Practical Theorist. New York, Basic Books, 1969
2. Smith ML, Glass GV, Miller TI: The Benefits of Psychotherapy. Baltimore, MD, Johns Hopkins University Press, 1980
3. Gabbard GO: Psychodynamic Psychiatry in Clinical Practice. Washington, DC, American Psychiatric Press, 1990
4. Mohl PC, Lomax J, Tasman A, et al: Psychotherapy training for the psychiatrist of the future. Am J Psychiatry 147:7–13, 1990
5. Perry S, Cooper AM, Michels R: The psychodynamic formulation: its purpose, structure, and clinical application. Am J Psychiatry 144:543–551, 1987
6. Davidovitz D, Levenson H: National survey on practice and training in brief therapy: comparison of psychologists, psychiatrists and social workers. Paper presented at the annual meeting of the American Psychological Association, New York, August 1995
7. Garfield SL: Research on client variables in psychotherapy, in Handbook of Psychotherapy and Behavior Change, 3rd Edition. Edited by Garfield SL, Bergin AE. New York, Wiley, 1986, pp 213–256
8. Phillips LE: The ubiquitous decay curve: delivery similarities in psychotherapy, medicine and addiction. Professional Psychology: Research and Practice 18:650–652, 1987

9. Pekarik G, Wierzbicki M: The relationship between clients' expected and actual treatment duration. Psychotherapy 23:532–534, 1986

10. Howard KI, Kopta SM, Krause MS, et al: The dose-effect relationship in psychotherapy. Am Psychol 41:159–164, 1986

11. Koss MP, Shiang J: Research on brief psychotherapy, in Handbook of Psychotherapy and Behavior Change, 4th Edition. Edited by Bergin AE, Garfield SL. New York, Wiley, 1993

12. Bloom BL: Planned Short-Term Psychotherapy. Boston, Allyn and Bacon, 1992

13. Sifneos PE: Short-Term Dynamic Psychotherapy: Evaluation and Technique, 2nd Edition. New York, Plenum, 1987

14. Cummings NA: The dismantling of our health system: strategies for the survival of psychological practice. Am Psychol 41:426–431, 1986

15. Peake TH, Bordin CM, Archer RP: Brief Psychotherapies: Changing Frames of Mind. Beverly Hills, CA, Sage, 1988

16. Bauer GP, Kobos JC: Brief Therapy: Short-Term Psychodynamic Intervention. Northvale, NJ, Jason Aronson, 1987

17. Levenson H, Butler SF: Brief dynamic individual psychotherapy, in The American Psychiatric Press Textbook of Psychiatry, 2nd Edition. Edited by Hales RE, Yudofsky SC, Talbott JA. Washington, DC, American Psychiatric Press, 1994, pp 1009–1033

18. Burlingame GM, Fuhriman A, Paul S, et al: Implementing a time-limited therapy program: differential effects of training and experience. Psychotherapy: Theory, Research and Practice 26:303–312, 1989

19. O'Malley SS, Foley SH, Watkins SD, et al: Therapist competence and patient outcome in interpersonal psychotherapy of depression. J Consult Clin Psychol 56:469–501, 1988

20. Rounsaville BJ, O'Malley S, Folwy S, et al: Role of manual-guided training in the conduct and efficacy of interpersonal psychotherapy for depression. J Consult Clin Psychol 56:681–688, 1988

21. Levenson H, Speed J, Budman SH: Therapist's experience, training, and skill in brief therapy: a bicoastal survey. Am J Psychother 49:95–117, 1995

22. Budman SH, Gurman AS: Theory and Practice of Brief Psychotherapy. New York, Guilford, 1988

23. Bolter K, Levenson H, Alvarez W: Differences in values between short-term and long-term therapists. Professional Psychology: Research and Practice 4:285–290, 1990

████████████████████████████████████

CONSIDER THIS APPROACH FOR PATIENTS WHO:[1]

Demonstrate some degree of ego deficit or insufficiency; that is, they

- Are unable to be introspective
- Are alexithymic—meaning that they have difficulty naming, discussing, and modulating emotions (aggression can be a particular problem in patients for whom supportive therapy is suitable)
- Are unable to tolerate painful emotions and suffering
- Have poor object relations, with an absence of the capacity for mutuality and reciprocity
- Make prominent use of primitive defenses, such as projective denial and splitting
- Have difficulty trusting others
- May tend to somaticize rather than experience problems
- Are unable to deal with, acknowledge, or discuss productively transference

In addition to such "lower-functioning" patients, however, there is reason to believe that the techniques of supportive therapy may also be suitable for a wide range of patients in an era of very brief, highly managed care.

---

[1] These selection criteria are adapted from the discussion of supportive therapy by Pinsker et al. (1).

SUPPORTIVE THERAPY: TREATMENT FOR LOWER-FUNCTIONING PATIENTS . . . AND OTHERS?

From the time he developed psychoanalysis to the end of his life, Freud was preoccupied with the criticism that psychoanalysis was merely "suggestion." Consequently, much of his writing reflects his insistence that true psychoanalysis was "gold," as compared with the "copper" of suggestion (2). This legacy in psychoanalysis led to an emphasis on the more "expressive" and technical aspects of psychoanalysis.

In traditional psychoanalysis, the patient engages in free association, saying anything and everything that comes to mind, while the quiet, listening analyst attempts to maintain a "neutral" stance. This neutrality was intended to prevent the analyst from revealing much about himself or herself. In the absence of information about the therapist, the patient's reactions to the therapist were expected to reflect, in a more or less pure fashion, the patient's conflicts with significant others in his or her past.

The resulting relationship was highly artificial and could be quite awkward and uncomfortable for patients to experience. Consider, for instance, the practice of some analysts to refuse to answer questions. Were the patient to ask, "Are you married?" the analyst might answer, "Do you think I am married?" or "Does it matter if I am married?" The tension and anxiety that resulted from such stilted interaction supposedly brought to the fore fantasy material to be interpreted. The goal was to make the unconscious conscious and to change the patient's personality structure.

The extremely rigid and restrictive stance of tradition has given way, even in psychoanalysis, to more flexibility and naturalness (3). Expressive techniques are still designed to bring into the patient's conscious awareness thoughts, feelings, and patterns of behavior of which he or she was hitherto unaware. This remains an anxiety-provoking experience and requires a patient who is very actively involved. A patient in expressive therapy must be willing and able to cooperate with the therapist in an admittedly peculiar interaction. The ability to acknowledge and discuss feelings and to invest at least some minimal level of trust in the therapist is essential for any expressive exploration. Finally, the defining technique of dynamic psychotherapy, namely, working with the patient's transference, requires the patient to be able to set aside his or her immediate feelings—for instance, of anger—and to consider how feelings toward the therapist might illuminate conflicts with others in the patient's current and past life.

Obviously, patients vary in their willingness and ability to engage in such a stylized interaction. Some patients (including therapists in therapy) can clearly engage in and benefit from anxiety-provoking techniques. Therapists have referred to these "ideal" patients as YAVIS (young, attractive, verbal, intelligent, and sophisticated). Other patients are essentially unable to participate in such a relationship. What, then, does dynamic therapy have to offer to these people?

As Luborsky (4) has pointed out in his classic manual on supportive-expressive therapy, most psychotherapies have supportive components, even the most expressive. Luborsky argues that patient characteristics determine the appropriate proportions of supportiveness versus expressiveness. The greater the psychiatric severity, the more supportive and less expressive the therapy may be. We tend to agree with Luborsky in this regard and believe that a predominantly supportive therapy can be a very effective and helpful treatment for many patients. In this chapter, we discuss therapy directed primarily toward the supportive end of the supportive-expressive continuum. However, given the increasing demand that therapy for all patients be extremely brief (six to eight sessions), the techniques of supportive therapy may become more in evidence, regardless of the functional status or psychotherapy potential of the patient.

Our presentation here relies greatly on the work of Pinsker et al. (1) at the Beth Israel Psychotherapy Research Program to characterize the specific techniques of supportive psychotherapy. These authors have made the contribution of articulating components of psychotherapy that have long been ignored in the psychodynamic literature, and yet supportive therapy remains the kind of treatment that is most likely provided to most psychiatric patients in this country.

■ DEFINITION OF SUPPORTIVE PSYCHOTHERAPY

In contrast to the overall objective of expressive psychotherapy, namely, to bring about personality change, Pinsker et al. (1) define supportive psychotherapy in this way:

> Individual dynamic supportive psychotherapy is a dyadic treatment characterized by use of direct measures to ameliorate symptoms and to maintain, restore, or improve self-esteem, adaptive skills, and ego function. (p. 221)

Such a definition does not rule out the therapist's attention to transference issues. The therapist continues to monitor "allusions to the transference" (see Chapter 5) as a way of monitoring and managing the state of the patient-therapist relationship. Appropriate transference gratification is another hallmark of supportive therapy (5). Finally, in contrast to more expressive therapy, the major focus of supportive therapy is current circumstances. The focus of supportive therapy is often on the immediate problems that have brought the patient to treatment. Thus, the focus of treatment for a patient who is chronically depressed is not on securing changes within the personality that contribute to the chronic depression, but rather to ameliorate the current deterioration in functioning and return the patient to his or her baseline. Although this goal may appear to be modest, our experience and some empirical work suggests that one should not underestimate the power of supportive interventions for patients' long-term adjustment.

■ SELECTION OF PATIENTS

Although there is little controversy regarding the use of supportive techniques with low-functioning patients, therapists have been less comfortable with the use of supportive techniques for higher-functioning patients, for whom expressive therapy has been the traditional treatment of choice (1). It is our opinion that the responsible therapist must take a practical stand, holding the interests of the patient as the paramount deciding factor. Rather than relying solely on patient characteristics, it is vital to take into account the resources available for the current round of therapy.

For a talented patient who is interested in personality exploration and change and who has the resources, a decidedly expressive therapy approach is warranted. Indeed, as is discussed in Chapter 5 ("Time-Limited Dynamic Psychotherapy"), much can be done with a willing patient in a relatively brief period (20–25 sessions). Some patients, however, have very limited insurance coverage, and it may be most responsible for the therapist to focus, in a supportive way, on the immediate concerns that have brought that patient to therapy, regardless of the patient's potential for therapy. This blurs further the traditional demarcation between patients who are suitable for the "gold" of expressive therapy from the lower-functioning, ego-deficit patients who must make do with the so-called inferior "copper" of supportive therapy.

■ GOALS OF TREATMENT

Setting explicit goals is of central importance for supportive therapy, as is true of all approaches to relatively brief treatment. Coming to an agreement on an agenda for treatment permits the patient to have a sense of control in the relationship and can reduce anxiety by making the therapeutic process less uncertain and less unfocused. Often the patient clearly articulates the overall goal by a statement such as "I want to stop being depressed." It is the therapist's job to formulate the dynamics of the patient's symptoms or current difficulties and to begin to make connections with issues such as self-esteem and adaptive functioning. The therapist should be able to convey the connections between the issues to be discussed and the patient's overall goals, which must be realistic. Rather than a total elimination of symptomatology in a chronically symptomatic patient, Pinsker et al. (1) recommend goals such as the following:

- The patient should acquire the ability to understand the connection between his or her problems and poor self-esteem and/or lack of adaptive skills.
- The patient should understand how various symptoms, behaviors, or feelings are manifestations of his or her problems with self-esteem and poor adaptive skills.
- The patient should gain control of strategies for coping with his or her problems.

Change, therefore, is not the result of resolution of unconscious conflicts. Rather, change arises from learning and through identification with an "accepting, well-related therapist" (1, p. 226). Supportive therapy seeks to improve patients' lives by directly striving for improved self-esteem and acquisition of better adaptive skills. Poor self-esteem tends to be associated with helplessness, demoralization, and an unwillingness to try new ways of dealing with problems. In the context of a good (though uninterpreted) relationship with a therapist, the patient's self-esteem can improve, increasing openness to learning new skills. Rather than attempting to remove defenses through interpretation, supportive therapy strives to correct distorted perceptions of self and others through education. In summary, the good outcome in supportive therapy is "increased self-esteem, reduction in experienced anxiety or dysphoria, and a resultant stabilization or increase in adaptive functioning" (1, p. 227).

■ THE THERAPEUTIC ALLIANCE

Considerable psychotherapy research confirms the central place of the therapeutic alliance in achieving a positive outcome (6). In supportive therapy, the role of the therapeutic alliance is especially emphasized and is enhanced through the use of accurate empathic responses, validation of feeling states, respectful and warm attitude, reassurance, and other overt and conventional efforts to establish a good relationship. Positive transference is not interpreted but is accepted as evidence that a positive alliance is developing.

Negative transference can threaten the therapeutic alliance, and the therapist must be alert to its emergence. With higher-functioning patients, detailed examination and clarification of the negative feelings and identification of their source can be constructive. This approach, however, requires patients to possess the skills to separate the negative feelings from the immediate interpersonal context and to examine those feelings. To explore and talk about strong, negative feelings with the person to whom those feelings are directed is a very high-level skill that certain patients may simply be unable to do. With lower-functioning patients, the therapist should consider changing his or her stance, as one might when talking with someone who is becoming angry or distant in a social setting.

■ TECHNIQUES OF SUPPORTIVE THERAPY

In this section we present a list of the techniques outlined by Pinsker et al. (1), who present these technical considerations as applicable to both lower- and higher-functioning patients. Therapy with markedly impaired patients is more likely to involve the use of direct measures to improve self-esteem and functioning. Reassurance, praise, encouragement, and direct advice are examples of such direct measures, with the goal of developing more adaptive coping strategies and containing symptoms. Higher-functioning patients are more likely to spend time examining relationships, self-concept issues, and patterns of feeling and behaving.

Reducing Anxiety

The stance of the therapist is designed to reduce uncertainty and the anxiety that usually accompanies it. Patients who are beginning therapy are asked to open up in an unfamiliar and possibly threatening setting. The individual who may resist opening up to an intimate is now asked to spill all to a virtual stranger—in the stranger's office, on his or her turf. Such a patient may have thoughts such as "What could happen here? Will the therapist laugh at me or ridicule me? What if I talk about the wrong topic? What if I sound stupid?" Such concerns are particularly likely to inhibit insecure individuals seeking therapy.

The supportive therapy approach is to adopt a conversational style of relating to patients. This does not mean that the discussion is like ordinary conversation, because the therapist never takes the floor. However, appropriate questions are generally answered, a comment might be offered just to show that the therapist is listening, and interjections and comments are made as they might be in an ordinary social conversation in which one person is intent on hearing and understanding what the other person is saying. The therapist should avoid challenging or provoking the patient and should never make pronouncements such as "You feel such and such." It is often wise to couch an observation in qualifiers that allow the patient an "out." People generally respond well to an empathic, curious attitude on the part of an active listener.

Anxiety is also further reduced by increasing the patient's sense of control. One way to do this is for the therapist to explain what "we" are doing, allowing the patient to be prepared for what will happen. If the therapist is about to say something that might upset a patient, warning the patient that what is about to be said might be upsetting helps give the patient a measure of control, as does asking if the patient is willing to go on. This is analogous to informing patients of what comes next during a physical examination. The therapist should always be patient and respectful and should back off if the patient requests it or becomes upset.

Enhancing Self-Esteem

Many patients feel that they are to blame for their problems. They are sure that the world will judge them. Indeed, they typically judge themselves very harshly and readily expect others, including the therapist, to judge and reject them as well. With higher-functioning patients, it is useful to draw out such a pattern, especially in the transference, and point out, for instance, how their expectation of judgment and rejection obstructs their awareness that others do not, in fact, judge or reject them. With lower-functioning patients, a similar dynamic may apply, but they may be less able to recognize their ability to change such a pattern. With these patients, it may be more productive to empathize with the difficulties they have experienced. An example might be to say, "It must have been hard feeling rejected by your father." (Some therapists—for example, Mann—use empathizing with difficulties faced by higher-functioning patients to foster nondefensive collaboration; see Chapter 3.)

It is particularly important to avoid criticism and to recognize that a patient with low self-esteem is hypersensitive to criticism. Naturally, if one feels bad about oneself, it is easy to imagine that others see oneself in the same way. The therapist should be aware, however, that this can present nearly impossible dilemmas. It is difficult to find a way to talk about improving something in someone's life without the implication that he or she has done something wrong. This quandary can be addressed directly with higher-functioning patients. With lower-functioning patients, it often best, as described above, to focus on the empathic response. Statements that most people, even the self-critical, can accept are those that merely observe their criticism of themselves, such as "You are really hard on yourself" or "It sounds like you don't often give yourself a break."

Finally, patients with low self-esteem often overemphasize their negative traits and underemphasize their positive qualities and accomplishments. Especially with lower-functioning patients, it is vital to explore their history for competencies and accomplishments. Pointing out such accomplishments and competencies must be done in a genuine way, but everyone has some area of competency that can be highlighted. The importance of being genuine cannot be overstated. Expert at minimizing any accomplishment, patients with low self-esteem will be on the lookout for any insincerity.

Respecting Defenses

In supportive therapy, adaptive defenses and the patient's personal style are generally respected. Defenses such as repression, reaction formation, rationalization, and intellectualization are generally encouraged, or at least are not challenged. When adaptive, denial, too, is compatible with good emotional health. Respect for the patient's defenses means, in part, not challenging them from the outset. The patient who says, "I don't want to think about it," may be expressing how he or she adaptively deals with a particular topic. A follow-up such as, "Does it work to avoid thinking about it?" gives the patient a chance to consider the effectiveness of the defense.

Supportive therapy does not encourage what are considered to be maladaptive or pathological defenses. Regression is typically not an adaptive response to life's problems. Defenses such as projection, splitting, maladaptive denial, and grossly unrealistic planning should be confronted. Some lower-functioning patients, for instance, deny that they have mental problems that require medication. One low-functioning patient decided to apply for a position as a "Bosnian mercenary." Such defenses are rarely adaptive.

The admonition to respect the patient's defenses remains, however, even with unacceptable defenses. A defense is so named because it serves some psychic purpose. Ignoring this fact will lead to therapeutic failure. The therapist should always avoid arguing with the patient. It may be useful for the therapist to tell the patient that he or she is concerned and does not understand how not taking medication will help. The exploration should always be respectful of the purpose the defense serves, even if it is not immediately apparent.

Clarification, Confrontation, and Interpretation

Clarification, confrontation, and interpretation are technical maneuvers that are also an integral part of expressive therapy. In supportive therapy, however, the purpose is not to make the unconscious conscious. Clarification is used to summarize, paraphrase, and organize the patient's statements without elaboration or inference. Clarification provides evidence that the therapist is listening and understands what the patient is communicating. It can be used to improve the patient's understanding of the situation. Confrontation brings to the patient's attention something the patient is avoiding or not attending to. In supportive therapy, this is usually conducted in a specific context, like increasing some adaptive skill. Even the most supportive therapy has the goal of increasing the patient's understanding of behavior patterns that are causing ongoing problems. Confrontation around projective blaming of others—for instance, rationalizing inactivity, denied anger, or an unrealistic sense of entitlement—might help the patient sort out cause-and-effect connections that account for some of his or her problems. In this context, interpretations generally refer to making explicit the connections elicited by clarification and confrontations.

The tone and style of such a discussion are important. In anxiety-provoking expressive therapy, a patient's chronic vagueness might be challenged. In supportive therapy, a vague patient might be urged to be more specific. As Pinsker et al. (1) point out, the goal of supportive therapy is not to explore the motivation underlying a personality style such as "vagueness," but rather to facilitate the patient's ability to communicate more effectively. Interpretations that make reference to primitive, libidinal impulses are never warranted.

Rationalization

Although rationalization is a defense, not a technique, Pinsker et al. (1) list it as one of the tools that can be used by a supportive therapist. Rationalization is a common way in which people explain why they end up doing the things they do and not doing other things. Rationalization accounts for actions (or lack of actions) without necessarily providing an understanding the "true" motivation that might be uncovered during formal psychoanalysis.

For example, consider the decision to go to medical school. A young man might overcome some ambivalence by rationalizing that becoming a physician is a respected and well-paid profession. In psychoanalysis, however, it could emerge that his "true" motivation is an oedipal wish to "beat" and humiliate a harsh father by attaining greater social and economic status than he did, along with the wish to gain the admiration of the mother that the father never could.

A historical bias has favored a psychoanalytic insistence on uncovering one's "true" motivations. As a result, therapists have been reluctant to foster rationalization or any other defense. More modern approaches recognize that some defenses can be used therapeutically. In the above example, if the young man's uncomfortable ambivalence is resolved with rationalization, perhaps this is enough understanding. As with all psychotherapeutic techniques, the use of rationalization cannot be superficial. Any rationalization that is offered must hold personal meaning for the particular patient in order to be effective.

Reframing

Pinsker et al. (1) list reframing as a useful technique to help patients improve their self-esteem and adapt more effectively. Reframing can allow the patient to see an issue from a different perspective that, in turn, permits new and different actions and ways of looking at the issue.

Consider, for instance, the case of a young man referred to treatment for violating his wife's restraining order. Exploration reveals that his increasing frustration is an extension of the control he desired to have in the relationship. Although he is unable to directly acknowledge and work with his pathological need to control others, he is responsive to a reframing of his need to regain control by staying away from his wife. He is thus able to see that violating the restraining order is not increasing his control of the situation. Instead, as the police and courts increasingly "take her side," he is steadily losing more and more control of the situation. Reframing adherence to the restraining order as a method of gaining control permits the therapist to help this patient adopt a more adaptive coping strategy. Thus, although the personality pathology is not directly addressed, the patient is able to obey the restraining order and stay away from his wife.

Encouragement

Encouragement, reassurance, and praise are ways in which people support each other. Stereotypic views of dynamic therapy have resulted in many therapists being reluctant to "flatter the patient" or to "feed the narcissism" (7, p. 151). Supporting self-esteem and adaptive coping, however, is an integral part of supportive therapy.

Although praise may reinforce certain behaviors, such encouragement or praise should not be confused with the operant behaviorist's use of praise as a "reinforcer." In dynamically oriented supportive therapy, praise and encouragement are not used to reinforce certain behaviors. Rather, praise and encouragement should be genuine expressions from the therapist that will communicate goodwill to the patient and facilitate the therapeutic alliance. As this implies, praise must be based on facts and directed toward something the patient considers meaningful. Insincere or manipulative praise will be detected by the patient and may foster suspicion that the therapist is presenting a false front. Such a perception runs the risk of damaging rather than strengthening the alliance.

Reassurance also has the direct effect of reducing anxiety. However, this, too, must be expressed in terms that are meaningful to the patient and should always be based on fact. Reassurance should not unrealistically promise that "things will get better," and the therapist should stick to areas of expertise or knowledge. Reassurance on some situation for which the therapist has no real insight (e.g., legal concerns) is unlikely to be reassuring.

In general, the use of overt encouragement, praise, and reassurance should probably be used sparingly. Such direct positive statements can be very effective coming from a therapist or other authority figure, such as a physician. This impact stems in part from the fact that such statements are unexpected. Overuse of such statements will water down the impact and, at worst, may create concerns in the patient's mind about the therapist's sincerity. A therapist whose credibility is lost will be ineffective.

Advising

Giving advice is something that many therapists learn explicitly not to do. Indeed, there are good reasons to avoid giving advice, the most important of which is that most people with problems typically receive all kinds of advice from family and friends. In most cases, the primary service that a therapist has to offer is to listen and reflect; that is, the therapist should do what other people do not do.

The prohibition against offering advice can be modified for lower-functioning patients. Certain patients have trouble with virtually every aspect of daily life, and some of these areas may fall within the scope of therapy. Pinsker et al. (1) suggest that advice is relevant if it is designed to help the patient act in ways that will enhance self-esteem, improve adaptive skills, or improve ego functioning. They recommend that the basis and rationale for any advice should be stated. Thus, a statement such as "You should work" should be avoided in favor of something like "Most people who stop working don't feel better—not working protects you from some stress, but it's usually bad for self-esteem." As with encouragement, praise, and reassurance, the therapist should be speaking as an expert, not as an authority.

Rehearsal or Anticipation

A technique that can help patients deal effectively with new and stressful situations is to anticipate and rehearse such situations. In the safety of the therapist's office, patients can rehearse what they want to say to, for example, a boss about some reprimand, or during a necessary meeting with an abusive ex-spouse. Patients can run through some future event and thereby reduce anticipatory anxiety associated with such events. Rehearsal further allows patients to directly adopt and practice new and unfamiliar coping strategies. It also can provide a forum for discussing their anticipated reactions or various approaches they might take. For instance, rehearsing a job interview with a very shy patient can reveal to both the patient and the therapist the patient's expectation of failure and the influence of this on how he or she "comes across" in the interview situation.

Responding to Ventilation

In a sense, one of the most valuable services that verbal therapies offer is the opportunity for an individual to ventilate. Reflection will confirm that there are really very few times in ordinary social intercourse when one can sit with another person and "get it all off one's chest." Many times, patients bring to therapy a sad or traumatic story that they have never been able to really tell anyone. By actively listening, the therapist can deepen the experience of ventilation. Such active responses include tracking (making comments or asking questions that show the therapist is following the patient's story), universalizing (making it clear that many people have similar feelings, wishes, or problems), and decatastrophizing (identifying where a patient may have exaggerated problems or issues and offer a more proportioned interpretation).

Attention to, Not Interpretation of, Transference

Transference holds a central position in the theory and practice of dynamic psychotherapy. What distinguishes dynamic supportive therapy from any other version of supportive therapy is the recognition that transference affects the patient's communications. This is as true for lower-functioning patients as it is for higher-functioning patients. Toward the expressive end of the continuum, allusions to the transference lead to exploration and possibly interpretation. Toward the supportive end, such allusions from lower-functioning patients inform the therapist about what is on the patient's mind but is hard for him or her to articulate. These insights can help the therapist guide the discussion, but these allusions generally should not be explored as they would be in expressive therapy. In the following case example, the therapist detects a rather extreme allusion to the transference from a young schizophrenic man.

Case Example

A therapist has been working with a schizophrenic man for about 2 years, on both an inpatient and an outpatient basis. The therapist is now moving to another part of the country. During their last session, the schizophrenic man begins the session by saying:

Patient: I'm a banana.
Therapist: Tell me about bananas.
Patient: They hang around all day and don't do anything all day long.
Therapist: Anything else?
Patient: You take off their skin and eat what's inside. When you're done with them, you throw them away.
Therapist: It's hard that I'm leaving, isn't it?
Patient: Yeah, that's it. I don't know who I'll have to talk to.

This low-functioning patient, who was not actively psychotic at the moment, was having feelings that he could not express. His "banana" comment is at first indecipherable but with some questioning emerges clearly as an allusion to thoughts and feelings about the therapist that he had difficulty expressing. The therapist used the insight gained from the realization that the comment referred to what was happening in the here-and-now and was able to move the conversation quickly in a more overt and productive direction.

Conclusion

The supportive techniques outlined here and listed in Table 2–1 are presented for use largely with lower-functioning patients. However, these techniques are equally suitable for higher-functioning patients, especially in a very brief therapy format. Such techniques are good adjuncts to any therapeutic stance or approach.

The experienced therapist knows, however, that techniques are not, in and of themselves, supportive or even effective. The effect of any particular technical maneuver is a direct result of the meaning that technique has for the individual patient (8). What one

TABLE 2–1. Techniques of supportive dynamic psychotherapy	
Reducing anxiety	Encouragement
Enhancing self-esteem	Advising
Respecting defenses	Rehearsal or anticipation
Clarification, confrontation, and interpretation	Responding to ventilation
Rationalization	Attention to, not interpretation of, transference
Reframing	

Source. Adapted from Pinsker H, Rosenthal R, McCullough L: "Dynamic Supportive Therapy," in *Handbook of Short-Term Dynamic Psychotherapy*. Edited by Crits Christoph P, Barber JP. New York, Basic Books, 1991, pp. 220–247. Copyright © 1991 by Basic Books, Inc. Used with permission of Basic Books, a division of HarperCollins Publishers, Inc.

patient experiences as supportive another might see as condescending, manipulative, or negative in some other way.

For example, two patients might successfully complete some task like registering for a class. One might easily accept praise for this from the therapist, whereas the other reacts with shame, saying, in essence, "Anyone should be able to register for a class." The therapist who assumes that praise, or any particular technique, is universally supportive will miss important information. Tracking such reactions to what the therapist does is a vital skill for any therapist.

The following vignette is excerpted from the work of Pinsker et al. (1) and illustrates some supportive techniques.

■ CLINICAL ILLUSTRATION

The patient is a young woman who began treatment because she was depressed and felt dissatisfied with her life. As therapy has progressed, it has become clear that she judges herself as indecisive and uncertain about everything. In this session the patient discussed having taken a second job, a night job at a bar, which she quit after a few days.

Patient: At first I felt bad to start and quit. It wasn't as good as I thought it was going to be, and I was very tired the next day. It's more important I do well at my regular job.

Therapist [Clarifies]: You felt bad about quitting, but only a little bad.

Patient: Yeah. I felt a little bad because I could make money if I stuck it out, but I realized it was going to be hard. If people stayed late, I'd have to stay, too. And they wanted me to work on nights when I had school.

Therapist [Asks for confirmation of his understanding of the patient's statements]: Well, would I be correct if I said that you still think an extra job to make some money is a good idea, but that this is not the way to do it?

Patient: I just realized I didn't have time for school. The best thing about it is that now I value my time more. After that, now my schedule seems great.

Therapist [Fact-based praise]: Well, you made this decision without a lot of uncertainty.

Patient: No, I was pretty sure.

Therapist [Asks for feedback about accuracy of praise]: It sounds to me like taking the job was a reasonable thing to do, and getting out as soon as you saw that it wasn't good was also a reasonable thing to do. Would you agree?

Patient: Yeah.

Therapist [Reminds patient of their agenda and attempts to enhance self-esteem by reinforcing patient's aware-ness of good adaptive function]: Since I'm always coming back to the issue of self-confidence—what did

it do for your self-confidence that you made a decision
to do it and then you made a decision to stop doing it?

Patient: Yeah, it was OK. At first I thought I was copping
out because I didn't think I'd be able to handle it, but
by the third night, I was catching on . . . so last week
was a tough week.

Therapist [Makes empathic conversational response]: It
sure sounds like it!

This short vignette illustrates the use of some of the techniques
described in this chapter. Note the cautious way in which the
therapist phrases his questions, which reflects his attempt to not
take anything for granted. The goal is to gain an understanding of
what the patient is saying that is as complete as possible. The
therapist also demonstrates how to check in with the patient after
using a technique such as praise in order to ensure that he and the
patient agree on the meaning of what has just transpired.

■ EMPIRICAL FINDINGS

Until recently, supportive therapy was not considered a separate
kind of therapy. As discussed earlier, most of the focus in dynamic
therapy is on expressive therapy, with the assumption that supportive therapy could certainly be done by an accomplished expressive
therapist. Psychotherapy research on dynamic therapy has generally followed this principle, yielding few studies of a designated
supportive therapy. Psychotherapy research has, however, studied
extensively the role of the therapeutic alliance on outcome. Regardless of the kind of therapy being tested, the quality of the
therapeutic alliance tends to be associated with outcome (9). Supportive techniques have been shown to be at least as helpful as
drugs or other therapies, such as cognitive, behavioral, or insight-
oriented therapies, in patients with coronary artery disease (10),
opiate addiction (11), phobia (12), and "anxious depression" (13).

As Pinsker et al. (1) point out, the strongest evidence for the value of supportive therapy comes from two large studies: a study of treatment for chronic schizophrenia (14) and the study of severely disturbed, nonpsychotic patients conducted over 40 years at the Menninger Clinic (15). In both studies, contrary to expectations, supportive therapy was found to be at least as effective as expressive methods, and in some cases was more so. Indeed, the view of supportive therapy expressed by Pinsker et al. (1) and in this chapter reflects the empirical findings that severely disturbed patients are more likely to respond to supportive rather than expressive techniques.

■ RELEVANCE FOR MANAGED CARE

A time frame for brief, supportive therapy has been set at about 40 sessions by the Beth Israel Psychotherapy Research Program. Today, a time frame of 40 sessions may not be possible, because many managed care organizations often limit outpatient sessions to 20 or fewer. Our impression is that many of the techniques of supportive therapy outlined in this chapter can be extraordinarily useful within any number of sessions. Even in the context of a single session, techniques to reduce anxiety, enhance self-esteem, and provide clarification can be beneficial to patients in distress. The hallmark of a supportive therapist is to be flexible with what the patient offers. This stance applies not only to the patient's characteristics but also to his or her mental health coverage.

■ REFERENCES

1. Pinsker H, Rosenthal R, McCullough L: Dynamic supportive therapy, in Handbook of Short-Term Dynamic Psychotherapy. Edited by Crits-Christoph P, Barber JP. New York, Basic Books, 1991, pp 220–247
2. Freud S: Line of advance in psychoanalytic therapy (1919), in The Standard Edition of the Complete Psychological Works of Sigmund Freud, Vol 17. Translated and edited by Strachey J. London, Hogarth Press, 1955, pp 157–168

3. Gabbard GO: Psychodynamic Psychiatry in Clinical Practice. Washington, DC, American Psychiatric Press, 1990

4. Luborsky L: Principles of Psychoanalytic Psychotherapy: A Manual for Supportive-Expressive Treatment. New York, Basic Books, 1984

5. Rockland LH: Supportive Therapy: A Psychodynamic Approach. New York, Basic Books, 1989

6. Henry WP, Strupp HH, Schacht TE, et al: Psychodynamic approaches, in Handbook of Psychotherapy and Behavior Change, 4th Edition. Edited by Bergin AE, Garfield SL. New York, Wiley, 1994, pp 467–508

7. Viederman M: The active dynamic interview and the supportive relationship. Compr Psychiatry 25:147–157, 1989

8. Butler SF, Strupp HH: "Specific" and "nonspecific" factors in psychotherapy: a problematic paradigm for psychotherapy research. Psychotherapy 23:30–40, 1986

9. Winston A, Pinsker H, McCullough L: A review of supportive psychotherapy. Hosp Community Psychiatry 37:1105–1114, 1986

10. Razin AM: Psychosocial intervention in coronary artery disease: a review. Psychosom Med 44:363–387, 1982

11. Woody GE, Luborsky L, McLellan AT, et al: Psychotherapy for opiate addicts. Monographs of the National Institute of Drug Abuse Research 43:59–70, 1983

12. Klein DF, Zitrin CM, Woerner MG, et al: Treatment of phobias: behavior therapy and supportive psychotherapy: are there any specific ingredients? Arch Gen Psychiatry 40:139–145, 1983

13. Schwab JJ: Anxiety and depression. Clin Ther 6:536–545, 1984

14. Carpenter WT: A perspective on the psychotherapy of schizophrenia project. Schizophr Bull 10:599–603, 1984

15. Wallerstein RS: The psychotherapy research project of the Menninger Foundation: an overview. J Consult Clin Psychol 57:195–205, 1989

CONSIDER THIS APPROACH FOR PATIENTS WHO:

- Have individuation-separation issues
- Are young adults entering the developmental stage of identity versus role diffusion
- Are going through a complicated bereavement
- Have dependent-passive personality styles
- Have an adjustment disorder due to separation or loss (e.g., of status, ability, money, power)
- Have existential issues about the meaning of their lives

TIME-LIMITED THERAPY

■ BASIC FRAMEWORK

Birth ------------------------------------ Death

Focus on the line above from birth to death. Put an X where you think you are at the present time.

Now you are in the perfect frame of mind to comprehend James Mann's model of time-limited psychotherapy (TLP) (1, 2). Whereas other theorists have developed brief models out of economic necessity or clinical need in an era of managed care, tightening budgets, and waiting lists, TLP is based on using the structure of finite and limited time to help the patient confront difficulties in mastering separation anxiety.

In an almost poetic opening to his book, *Time-Limited Psychotherapy*, Mann (1) describes how folklore conveys limitless time and immortality in the figure of an abundant woman, whereas time as a limited commodity is represented by Father Time, with a beard and a scythe. He further states how a sense of timelessness is a part of a person's unconscious. He contrasts child time (subjective, eternal, endless) with adult time (objective, real, clock).

The reader can readily appreciate the difference between clock time (sundial to digital) and perceived time. With the latter, there are times when we are so bored or distressed that, as the refrain goes, "the moments seem like hours and the hours creep so slowly." At other times, usually in pleasurable situations, even days can seem to rush by in a blur.

TLP is psychodynamic in its basic philosophy and technique (e.g., use of conflict, resistance, transference, and interpretation), but it has a strong existential overlay:

> Although there is no effective means for struggling against time, we do try . . . . If one can eliminate time sense, one can also avoid the ultimate separation that time brings—death. (1, p. 6)

Mann sees that there is one basic human dilemma revolving around conflicts with separation-individuation. On the one hand, the person desires to be in a pleasurable state of timelessness where all needs are taken care of; on the other hand, one is painfully aware that time does pass and that one needs to make his or her own way. Dysfunction occurs when people cannot master or even tolerate the sense of separateness and autonomy and continue to act as if someday they will be rescued from their present state and no longer have to confront those issues.

■ THEORY AND TECHNIQUE

TLP is built around the aphorism "process follows structure." Mann (1) designed a time-limited structure for the therapy that ideally would activate the patient's anxiety regarding separation and loss and thus permit an examination and more successful resolution of his or her conflicts.

> Any psychotherapy which is limited in time brings fresh flame to the enduring presence in all persons of the conflict between timelessness, infinite time, immortality, and the omnipotent fantasies of childhood on the one hand, and time, finite time, reality, and death on the other hand. The wishes of the unconscious are timeless and promptly run counter to an offer of help in which time is limited. Thus, any time-limited psychotherapy addresses itself both to child time and to adult time. (1, pp. 10–11)

Mann's model of TLP is built on a tight structure of 12 sessions. Although Mann says that the 12 sessions can be distributed based on the patient's needs (e.g., a less well-functioning patient may be seen in weekly half-hour visits spread out over 24 weeks), most patients who are accepted for TLP are seen for the traditional 50-minute weekly session. (Mann admonishes practitioners not to call the 50-minute session an "hour": "This may appear to be an obsessional adherence to literalness. However, when the meaning of time is to be the lever that motivates and moves the patient, there is a sufficient mix of fantasy and reality without making for an unnecessary additional complication by calling a less than 60-minute meeting an hour" [1, p. 16].)

To the often-asked question, "Why 12 sessions?" Mann simply states that the number 12 is somewhat arbitrary, but that "experience has demonstrated that twelve treatment sessions is probably the minimal time required for a series of dynamic events to develop, flourish, and be available for discussion, examination, and resolution" (1, p. 15). In other words, it might take patients at least that amount of time to engage in the therapeutic relationship, experience the relationship, and then detach. Because the therapy is designed to heighten the conflicts between "realistic" individuation and "wishful" merger, it is critical that the patient have the sense of the passage of time in which there is a beginning, a middle, and an end. Mann and Goldman (2) point out that

> in all varieties of psychotherapy, the patient knows when therapy has begun, but he is seldom fully aware of the middle of treatment and usually does not recognize the end of treatment until the subject is explicitly discussed. In time-limited psychotherapy, the beginning, middle, and end are known from the start. (p. 10)

■ PHASES OF TREATMENT

Intake/Selection

Initially, an intake is performed, during which time historical data are obtained, the patient's psychological state is assessed, and a tentative diagnosis is given. One or two such evaluation meetings usually take place before TLP begins.

Table 3–1 lists the selection criteria for TLP. During the process of the initial interviews, the therapist ascertains a central issue or complaint. If the patient is so diffuse that such a central issue cannot be discerned, the therapist should consider the possibility of some psychotic thought process or a low motivation for change, either of which would signal that the patient is not appropriate for TLP.

Mann (1) reasons that young men and women who are developmentally facing the pressures of adulthood are particularly well suited to the focus and process of TLP. The most critical selection criterion, however, pertains to the individual's ability to rapidly attach and detach emotionally (i.e., tolerate loss) without decompensating (e.g., returning to a less mature defense, increasing

---

TABLE 3–1. **Selection criteria for patients receiving time-limited psychotherapy**

Inclusion criteria

    Capacity for rapid affective involvement and toleration of loss without serious disruption in functioning

    Adjustment disorders

    Neurotic character structure

Questionable status

    Obsessional characters (especially those with major defenses of isolation and intellectualization)

    Borderline patients

    Narcissistic disorders

    Psychosomatic disorders

Exclusion criteria

    Schizophrenia

    Bipolar affective disorders

    Schizoid disorders

---

symptoms). Areas important to know about in order to ascertain a patient's suitability for TLP include how he or she has handled previous losses, the occurrence of early deprivations, the ability to relate to the interviewer, and the capacity for affective expression. Despite these specifics,

> each patient, regardless of his presenting complaint and early history, must be evaluated on his own terms without any preconceived prejudice or bias . . . . [C]areful assessment of the patient's life history in terms of his relative success in work and in relationships with others becomes an effective means for determining suitability for time-limited psychotherapy. (2, pp. 61–62)

The "Honeymoon" Phase

The 3-month course of therapy can be conceptually divided into three phases, each approximately 1 month long. The first phase is aptly called the "honeymoon." After being accepted for TLP, the patient is told that his or her therapy will last 12 sessions, spread over 3 months. Mann gives the exact date of the last meeting to the patient and even takes out his calendar to dramatically underscore the significance and definiteness of the specific date. Theoretically, the adult part of the patient understands all of these strictures and realizes that 12 sessions is not a long time. The child portion of the patient, however, has the feeling that 3 months is very far in the future. It is not unusual for patients to "forget" how many sessions they have left and even to deny that they were told that therapy was to be time limited. Sometimes, however, the patient does ask whether 12 sessions will be enough. Mann sees such a question as stemming from a combination of the wish for endless time, the realistic awareness of calendar time, and the understanding of the time-limited nature of the therapy. He advises that if the patient is appropriate for TLP, the appropriate answer to the patient's question is a simple and "genuinely confident 'yes'" (1, p. 21).

In the honeymoon phase, the therapist is seen as the good and providing parent who will meet all needs and remedy past injustices; the therapeutic alliance is strong, positive, and unambivalent. During this phase, patients report a lessening of symptoms and an increase in hope in the process and faith in the therapist.

As early as possible, the therapist learns and then clarifies for the patient his or her central issue or major problem. Although patients usually come to therapy wanting treatment for specific symptoms (such as depression or anxiety), the TLP therapist seeks to discover the unconscious conflict that has resulted in these symptoms. In order to do so, the therapist must extract from the patient his or her "life story," which will reveal data about the patient's past and present situation, the occurrence of difficult or traumatic events, and the ways the patient learned to respond to these painful events. The therapist is looking for repetitive events and responses that reveal the patient's typical way of handling conflict.

The therapist's statement of the patient's central issue is most helpful to the patient (i.e., can be heard more openly and less defensively) if it emphasizes how the patient has attempted to cope with the unfairness and injustices of his or her life by developing certain ways of acting and reacting. Therapists should express the patient's life-long difficulties empathically, in terms of a "present and chronically endured pain" (i.e., recognizing that he or she has been victimized in some manner). In this way, the patient will feel supremely understood and nurtured by the therapist (further strengthening the already positive working alliance). According to TLP, this emphatic connection with the patient's pain should facilitate the patient's recognizing and processing unconscious conflicts. Table 3–2 outlines some of the ways in which the therapist can begin to ascertain the patient's central issue.

Negative Transference Phase

The second phase of treatment is the negative transference phase, which occupies the middle month of treatment. In this phase, the

---

TABLE 3–2. **How to choose a central issue**

---

1. Listen for themes in the patient's story that are evident in the past and continue into the present.

2. Look for actions by which the patient has mastered or adapted to difficult life circumstances (usually at great personal cost).

3. Examine how the patient keeps childhood struggles and attendant adult pain out of his or her awareness.

4. Note the patient's self-image.

5. Delineate issues clustering around one of four themes:

   a. Independence versus dependence

   b. Activity versus passivity

   c. Adequate versus diminished self-esteem

   d. Unresolved or delayed grief

TLP therapist is more directive and interpretative, linking repetitive patterns with underlying conflicts. With the passage of sessions, the patient realizes that miraculous changes in his or her life situations have not occurred; he or she has not been "cured." As if that weren't bad enough, the therapist is reminding the patient that the therapy is half over. Understandably, the patient reacts negatively.

It is important during this phase for the therapist to not personalize the patient's negative reactions and think that the therapy is going badly. In fact, it is critical from a TLP viewpoint that patients have a safe enough place to express these powerfully negative feelings that hearken back to disappointed feelings experienced (but often not expressed) with earlier (usually parental) figures in life. The therapist should invite an exploration of the patient's frustrated, ambivalent feelings, which might be overtly demonstrated through lateness, reemergence of symptoms, and outright complaints.

Termination Phase

The last, or termination, phase is critical in that it affords the patient the opportunity to separate in a less ambivalent, more mature, and more confident manner than has previously been the case. Patients will attempt to deal with the impending ending of the therapy and loss of the therapeutic relationship in their own characteristic manner, typical of how they dealt with previous separations. If the therapist can deal directly and explicitly with the patient's pain and fears about ending, the patient will have a greater chance of internalizing the understanding and accepting therapist as a replacement for earlier, disappointing parental figures:

> This time the internalization will be more positive (never totally so), less anger-laden, and less guilt-laden, thereby making separation a genuine maturational event. (1, p. 36)

Throughout all phases of TLP, it is crucial that the therapist stay focused on exploring the patient's central issue. In the first phase, keeping such a tight focus not only will permit a deeper understanding of those issues but also will prevent regression by restricting the scope of the work. In the middle phase, attending to the central issue keeps the patient focused despite his or her impatience—after all, from the patient's perspective, there are many important areas to discuss. This raises the patient's awareness of the conflicts embedded in the central issue—namely, that he or she, in characteristic fashion, is headed for yet another difficult separation without feeling whole. Similarly, in the last phase, the therapist discusses termination through the lens of the patient's central issue.

■ REVERBERATIONS FOR THE THERAPIST

Perhaps more than any other model of brief therapy, Mann's TLP is the most affect-laden for the therapist. Like their patients, therapists must confront their own conflicts regarding loss. In teaching this model, we have found that therapists who are inexperienced in providing brief therapy often find "very good reasons" for continuing the therapy and avoiding termination. Mann believes that it is these resistances to dealing with the separation that make for either extended, open-ended therapies or botched endings. Therapists who are attempting TLP should be particularly attentive to clearly communicating the termination date to patients, avoiding ambivalent communications regarding the request for more sessions (e.g., "We'll see") and reminding patients of the decreasing number of sessions.

■ CLINICAL ILLUSTRATION

The illustrative case example presented here (2) is that of Ms. A, a 40 year-old married woman with four school-age children who came for outpatient therapy because she feared she had cancer and did not have long to live. Ms. A had recently had a biopsy of a facial lesion. Although the most likely diagnosis was easily treated skin cancer, Ms. A felt that it was a surface indication of something fatal. Her history revealed multiple visits to physicians for a myriad of physical symptoms (e.g., headaches, stomach pains, burning sensations in arms and legs) for at least a decade.

In the intake interview, Ms. A indicated that she had been trained as a medical technician and was presently working in the same medical center where her father had died of a myocardial infarction at age 48. As a child, she had been concerned about his hypertension, and she talked about how she would listen for his snoring at night as a sign that he was still alive. Ms. A felt that she was a caregiver to her mother, although she acknowledged that her mother was rather independent. She was aware that she had a propensity to take care of others, which she then experienced as burdensome. Her husband seemed to be a good provider who was generally supportive of his wife of 13 years. Her earliest memory (about which she was unsure had really happened) was of being in a store with her parents at age 5 and becoming panicky when she found herself alone—abandoned.

As Ms. A continued to describe her present and past feelings and interactions with various family members, a theme emerged that she had an overpowering need to "do for" others while feeling unworthy herself. At the end of the first evaluation interview, Ms. A asked, "Do you think I can be helped?" to which the therapist replied, "Yes, but there is further information that I would like to have, and then I will suggest what we might do."

In the second evaluation interview, more historical information supported the therapist's hypothesis that Ms. A had a compulsive need to do good for others and that she felt undeserving herself because she became furious with her need to constantly give of herself with little gratifying return or recognition. Her anger must be tied, the therapist felt, to sadistic, guilt-provoking fantasies that increased her sense of unworthiness, which in turn increased her need to be good and to do for others. In addition, if she were not good, she feared she would be abandoned and unloved. This fear engendered anger, mobilizing guilt, which was mastered by further doing good. Thus, she was trapped in this sequence of affects (2).

The following dialogue illustrates how the therapist empathically presented the central issue to the patient in terms of her chronically endured pain in their second meeting.[1]

Therapist: You have always given of yourself to so many others, and yet you feel, and always have felt, both undeserving and unrewarded.
Patient: You mean by my husband?
Therapist: You feel unloved by him and all the others.
Patient: I often feel that I have no friends at all.

---

[1] Transcripted material is reprinted from Mann J, Goldman R: *A Casebook in Time-Limited Psychotherapy.* Northvale, NJ, Jason Aronson, 1991, pp. 81–98. Used with permission.

A treatment plan of 12 sessions, with a specific ending date, focusing on the central issue was agreed to by Ms. A. Before the hour ended, she spoke about how she had no self-confidence and relayed how she was beaten with a strap by her mother.

Later in this same session, the therapist reiterated the central issue to Ms. A:

> *Patient:* You know, I just remember again that memory or dream, whatever it is, about my parents abandoning me in the store.
>
> *Therapist:* You did to your little daughter what was done to you; you felt that you had abandoned her and you became sick.
>
> *Patient:* I never thought of that.
>
> *Therapist:* You have the need to be good out of fear that you will be left, unloved and uncared for.
>
> *Patient:* I don't want to go on with these thoughts about myself. I feel a churning inside; my arms and face feel like they are burning.
>
> *Therapist:* You are always ready to feel guilty.

The above vignette shows how the TLP therapist highlighted associative data from the patient's previous remarks to encourage her to make "intimate connections."

In the third session, the patient complained of a variety of symptoms, with renewed fears she might have cancer. Her therapist reminded her of the past session, in which she did not want to talk about her fear of being abandoned.

> *Patient:* There are times when I am afraid that my husband will leave me. I went to a meeting in which a lot of men were involved and I felt ignored, superfluous, and depressed. I told my husband about it and I cried. He said I was making too much of it.

Therapist: You were hurt by the men and then you became angry.

Patient: Now that you mention it, I was angry with those men even before the meeting. I knew how they would act with me.

Therapist: How must a woman feel who always has to please everyone of significance to her?

Patient: Frustration.

Therapist: Anger.

Patient: I suppose I give myself very little credit for anything.

Therapist: You are very hard on yourself. For example, you must feel apprehensive and tense here because of what you must feel are my expectations of you with so little time available.

Patient: I see that and I know that I am here to do something for myself and not for you . . . but what has all this to do with my symptoms?

Therapist: Your symptoms serve to avoid—to keep away from your awareness—your feelings, especially angry feelings.

Patient: Why?

Therapist: Let's ignore the "why" of it at this point and instead see how you have come to an automatic way of relating—to give and give in the hope of acceptance, and inevitably you come to suffer frustration and anger—that is what we should look at further.

Patient: What about my fear that I haven't long to live?

Therapist: We will have to wait on that. I know that this is all very difficult and painful for you.

Patient: Do you still think I can be helped?

Therapist: Yes.

In this third session, the therapist again helped the patient become aware of her feelings of anger in addition to those of hurt and frustration. The aspect of limited time was introduced. By the fourth session, the patient was feeling better—taking some risks with regard to her anger, independence, and anxiety. According to TLP, it is typical for patients to experience a decrease in symptoms during this honeymoon phase, but for this patient a lessening of complaints may also be a manifestation of her need to please.

The week before the fifth session was "awful"; the patient had felt angry with her husband. In the session, the therapist attempted to draw out the patient's transference feelings by suggesting that perhaps Ms. A was angry with the therapist for not giving her much time. The patient told him that she would be on vacation the next week. With such planned cancellations, the therapist can simply extend the termination date by another week. If cancellations become frequent, however, the therapist should explore the patient's conflicts about ending. If the patient simply did not show up for a session, the time would not be made up.

In the sixth session, Ms. A indicated that during her vacation she had felt irritable.

Therapist: You're experiencing a good deal of anger, and it must be something that you feel toward me.

Patient: I don't see why . . . .

Therapist: Well, you're feeling a good deal of pressure from me—so little time . . . .

Patient: What will happen to me if I feel no better at the end and you send me on?

Therapist: How much time do we have—how many sessions left?

Patient: I don't know.

Therapist: Guess.

Patient: Five.

Therapist: No, we still have six.

Patient: The pressure of time is always there.

Therapist: The pressure of time is really the pressure that you feel from people—from me—the pressure as to whether you can do it here.

Patient: It makes me angry. I am so much more aware of being angry . . . .

In the seventh session, the patient again underestimated the number of sessions left. Her therapist considered that this distortion was the product of her feeling that she was giving so much in the therapy and reaping so little benefit. Even if she had accurately remembered the number of sessions left, it is assumed that patients will find a way to express frustration and hopelessness midway in the therapy.

In the eighth session, the therapist reviewed with the patient how events in her life had resulted in her thinking that she was undeserving. In the ninth meeting, he interpreted to the patient that she did not want to leave him or for him to let her go. The patient agreed. In the 10th session, Ms. A talked about how she came to marry her husband.

Patient: Did I marry B. out of the feeling that I had to have someone who would put me down?

Therapist: In view of your relationship with the man who preceded your husband [a man who felt superior to her], and in the light of all that we have learned, it is likely that you could not have chosen someone who would have placed you on a pedestal.

Patient: You mean this thing about being undeserving?

Therapist: Yes.

Patient: Then my relationship with my husband can change only by changes that I make myself?

Therapist: Yes.

As the patient continued to talk about some symptoms she had experienced during the preceding week, her therapist connected her symptoms to her feelings about her father, his illness, and her guilt about his illness. The session concluded with Ms. A asking for an evaluation of her progress to this point. The therapist thought that the patient probably wanted him to tell her that he liked her and found her worthwhile.

In the 11th session, the therapist brought up termination, to which the patient replied that she had just come to accept the time limit and was not aware of any particular feelings toward him. She maintained this attitude until the topic of her deserving to live was raised.

Patient: I have always felt that my time is limited—that I would die young—and I still feel that way . . . (she begins to cry) . . . I'm afraid that it will all return after I'm through. What will I do?

Therapist: You mean then that I should not let you go.

Patient: At least if I knew I could come back to see you.

Therapist: We will talk some more about that next week.

In the last session, Ms. A, who had been relatively symptom free for 2 weeks, realized that the burning sensations in her skin happened when she was angry.

Therapist: You want me to tell you to stay?

Patient: No—I only want to know whether I can return if things go wrong.

Therapist: You are the kind of person who likes schedules and assurances. There are no guarantees in the task of living, and you will have to take your chances like the rest of us. Give yourself some time. I think that you will do all right, and if you come to feel that you need help, you'll know what to do.

The therapist then recapitulated what had been learned in the therapy about Ms. A's central issue and in the last minutes reminded her to maintain her self-esteem by being vigilant of her inferiority feelings and accomplishments.

In his earlier writings, Mann (1) indicated that it was important to have a real ending with the patient, to reinforce the idea that time was finite and losses occurred. Therefore, at the conclusion of the 12 sessions, the therapist was not supposed to see the patient again. (If the patient were not doing well at the end of the TLP, the therapist could take whatever steps were clinically indicated, such as referring her to another therapist or arranging for hospitalization or a different type of treatment, but the therapist would not extend the time he or she would personally treat the patient.)

In his later writings (2), Mann softened this prohibition against further therapeutic contact. The case of Ms. A is a good example. When Ms. A called her therapist 2 months after her last session, saying things were "quite bad," he promptly saw her for two additional sessions, focusing on her difficulties dealing with separation. Ms. A related a dream of how she does things for people and is abandoned nonetheless. The therapist replied that his ending the therapy did not mean that he did not care about her.

Approximately 6 months later, Ms. A called again, this time to say that she was doing well herself but wanted to work on her relationship with her husband. Subsequently, Ms. A and her husband were seen conjointly for four weekly sessions. The need for couple's work was a consequence of Ms. A's dealing more directly with her dissatisfaction with her husband. In the couple's sessions, both came to realize how they inflicted pain on the other rather than directly expressing their respective needs and wishes.

Mann concluded his summary of this difficult case by pointing out its complexities—such as the patient's long history of somatic preoccupations with multiple medical workups. He concluded that Ms. A had made marked gains in TLP, particularly with regard to an increase in functioning (both personally and socially) and self-esteem and a diminishment of her harsh, self-punitive thoughts, although she continued to struggle with her conflicts.

■ EMPIRICAL FINDINGS

Most investigations of the clinical effectiveness of TLP have been based on clinical case reports like that of Ms. A. The empirical outcome studies (3–5) have suggested that for highly selected patients, TLP results in significant therapeutic gains (symptom reduction, improved social functioning, increased self esteem) that are maintained for up to 2 years after termination. Preliminary results from one study (3), however, suggest that TLP patients may not encounter a negative transference phase in the middle of treatment, as proposed by the model.

■ RELEVANCE FOR MANAGED CARE

The perspective of managed care is consistent with the 12 sessions of TLP and its philosophical emphasis on making the most of limited time. However, managed care would be at variance with TLP's exploring the patient's central issue, which is thought to underlie the development of symptoms. In addition, the model in managed care today views the therapist as a resource for the patient, who can see him or her for intermittent therapy throughout his or her life, much like the family practitioner. This viewpoint is inconsistent with TLP's more rigid stance regarding the definitive ending of the therapeutic relationship.

Because TLP is best for higher-functioning patients, it may be useful only for a small percentage of people seeking help in a managed care setting. However, this existential approach could be very helpful for healthier patients whose passivity and dependency on the medical care system are manifestations of their inability to separate from caregivers (whether real or longed for). In this regard it seems ideally suited for patients who are symptomatic because of difficulties in dealing with separation.

■ REFERENCES

1. Mann J: Time-Limited Psychotherapy. Cambridge, MA, Harvard University Press, 1973
2. Mann J, Goldman R: A Casebook in Time-Limited Psychotherapy. Northvale, NJ, Jason Aronson, 1991
3. Joyce A, Piper WE: An examination of Mann's model of time-limited individual psychotherapy. Can J Psychiatry 35:41–49, 1990
4. Shefler G, Dasberg H, Ben-Shakhar G: A randomized controlled outcome and follow-up study of Mann's time-limited psychotherapy. J Consult Clin Psychol 63:585–593, 1995
5. Witztum E, Dasberg H, Shefler G: A two-year follow-up of time limited brief therapy in a community mental health center in Jerusalem. Isr J Psychiatry Relat Sci 26:244–258, 1989

CONSIDER THIS APPROACH FOR PATIENTS WHO:

Are given a diagnosis of depression, particularly if they are

- Going through a role transition (e.g., divorce, retirement, leaving home, illness)
- Experiencing overt or covert conflicts with a significant other (usually accompanied by feelings that nothing can be done or there are irreconcilable differences)
- Having abnormal grief reactions (i.e., not progressing through the various phases of the normal mourning process)
- Evidencing social isolation with or without deficiencies in social skills

4

INTERPERSONAL PSYCHOTHERAPY FOR PATIENTS WITH DEPRESSION

The assumption underlying interpersonal psychotherapy (IPT) is that clinical symptoms occur in "an interpersonal context and that psychotherapeutic interventions directed at this interpersonal context will facilitate the patient's recovery" (1, pp. 5–6). Although interpersonal difficulties may not be the sine qua non for producing emotional problems, they are strongly intertwined with them. For example, difficulties in interpersonal relations in childhood (e.g., loss of a parent, family discord, abuse) are strongly predictive of adult depression. In turn, adult depression is strongly correlated with further interpersonal difficulties (e.g., emotional dependency, withdrawal, interpersonal friction).

Although IPT was developed as a focused, time-limited treatment (14–18 weekly sessions) for depression, its strategies and principles have been modified for use in dealing with other psychiatric problems (2, 3). In this chapter, we present the application of IPT for its most common target syndrome—depression. In particular, IPT is especially useful in the treatment of depressed individuals who have medical illnesses. For this chapter's clinical illustration, we consider the topic of IPT with depressed HIV-positive outpatients.

IPT initially evolved from the New Haven–Boston Collaborative Depression Research Project. A book, *Interpersonal Psychotherapy of Depression* (1), was derived from the training manual and provides a good, practical resource for clinical practitioners who are interested in learning how to implement IPT in their own practices. This chapter highlights the major tenets from that book and presents current empirical data and more recent clinical applications. In addition, there is now an IPT guide for patients (4).

■ BASIC PRINCIPLES

Klerman et al. (1) state that IPT is not a "new" psychotherapy because many of its concepts and techniques are part of the standard armamentarium of psychodynamically trained therapists. However, IPT does systemize and operationalize an approach to the treatment of depression. Table 4–1 compares IPT with other, noninterpersonally focused, dynamic therapies. As is seen from Table 4–1, IPT focuses on 1) interpersonal relations (social roles and interactions among people) versus object relations or intrapsychic phenomena, 2) role expectations and disputes versus internal conflicts and wishes, and 3) here-and-now transactions versus childhood or past experiences.[1]

■ SELECTION CRITERIA

Klerman et al. (1) have very little to say about who is a suitable candidate for IPT for depression. (The entry *Selection* does not even appear in their book's index.) The original treatment was developed for nonpsychotic, nonbipolar, depressed outpatients.

---

[1] Because of these differences between IPT and other dynamic therapies, there is some difference of opinion regarding whether IPT is basically psychodynamic in its orientation (5; J. C. Markowitz, personal communication, August 1996). We have included it in this volume because 1) most practitioners of IPT have psychodynamic backgrounds, 2) IPT is consistent with many of the tenets of the interpersonal psychodynamic school, and 3) it is often so categorized by others (e.g., 6).

TABLE 4–1. Comparison of interpersonal psychotherapy with other psychotherapies

Interpersonal psychotherapy	Noninterpersonal psychotherapy
What has contributed to this patient's depression right now?	Why did the patient become what he or she is, and/or where is the patient going?
What are the current stresses?	What was the patient's childhood like?
Who are the key persons involved in the current stress? What are the current disputes and disappointments?	What is the patient's character?
Is the patient learning how to cope with the problem?	Is the patient cured?
What are the patient's assets?	What are the patient's defenses?
How can I help the patient ventilate painful emotions—talk about situations that evoke guilt, shame, and resentment?	How can I find out why this patient feels guilty, ashamed, or resentful?
How can I help the patient clarify his or her wishes and have more satisfying relationships with others?	How can I understand the patient's fantasy life and help him or her gain insight into the origins of present behavior?
How can I correct misinformation and suggest alternatives?	How can I help the patient discover false or incorrect ideas?

Source. Reprinted from Klerman GL, Weissman MM, Rounsaville BJ, et al: *Interpersonal Psychotherapy of Depression.* New York, Basic Books, 1984. Copyright © 1984 by Gerald L. Klerman, Myrna M. Weissman, Bruce J. Rounsaville, and Eve S. Chevron. Used with permission of Basic Books, a division of HarperCollins Publishers, Inc.

The originators of IPT do state that the brief time interval of IPT may not be sufficient for patients for whom depression is severe, there have been many previous episodes, the time between episodes has been short, and the social consequences of relapse are great. Research (7) has indicated that for patients, particularly males, social adjustment, interpersonal sensitivity, and social satisfaction are positively related to the benefits derived from IPT.

Patients taking antidepressant medication do not need to be excluded from receiving IPT. In fact, data indicate that there may be a synergistic effect between IPT and medication that results in a better outcome than would be expected by simply adding the effectiveness of each treatment independently. (See the section "Empirical Findings" later in this chapter.)

■ GOALS

The two major goals of IPT are 1) improvement in interpersonal functioning and 2) symptom reduction (e.g., elimination of early-morning awakening, lack of appetite). The overall aim of IPT is to solve problems within a brief period rather than to devise lifetime solutions, and its emphasis is on restoring the patient to an adequate level of functioning rather than on personality change. In this regard, IPT has much in common with supportive therapies (see Chapter 2); however, it also tends to be more active and ambitious than supportive therapies.

■ STRATEGIES AND PHASES OF TREATMENT

Specific tasks or strategies for IPT are divided into three phases: 1) initial sessions, 2) intermediate phase, and 3) termination phase.

Initial Sessions

In the first couple of sessions of IPT, an assessment is made of the diagnosis of depression through a review of the patient's symptoms. The therapist identifies one or two types of interpersonal problems most related to the patient's current depression by obtaining information about recent changes in the patient's life circumstances, mood, and social functioning. The four primary problem areas most frequently encountered by depressed people are

1. Grief
2. Interpersonal disputes (e.g., with spouse, children, or co-workers)
3. Role transitions (e.g., leaving home, becoming ill, loss of job)
4. Interpersonal deficits (e.g., social isolation, poor social skills)

For some patients, treatment may combine several of these principal problem areas. The therapist providing IPT helps the patient to understand the key types of problems he or she is having and the goals specific to those problems. (See the section "Intermediate Phase," below.) In most cases, the patient and the therapist agree on an appropriate focus for the therapy. For example, the therapist might say,

> It seems from what you have been telling me that you have been [state the current problem or problems clearly; e.g., having trouble in your marriage, arguing with your spouse, afraid of losing your job, uncomfortable in your new apartment, lonely in the city, missing your old friends, etc.]. These problems can certainly be related to your depression. I'd like to meet with you over the next few weeks, as we have been doing, for about an hour each time, to see if we can figure out how you can better cope with the situation. (1, p. 89)

Sometimes the patient and the therapist do not agree on the focus. Patients may be unwilling or unable to acknowledge certain problems or their reactions to them because the issues feel too threatening. For example, a patient may be reluctant to recognize that a spouse of 2 years has significantly different ideas about how they should spend their money (interpersonal dispute) because of fears that the spouse will leave if the patient asserts personal opinions. When there is disagreement on the focus for treatment, the therapist can 1) postpone goal-setting until the patient is more receptive; 2) initially set general goals, with the idea of becoming more specific as the therapy proceeds; or 3) go with what the patient thinks is significant, with the hope that once this is dealt with, the more central problem area can be addressed.

In addition to ascertaining the focus of the treatment, the initial phase also includes informing the patient that he or she has an illness because he or she is evidencing the signs and symptoms of the clinical syndrome of depression. This "sick role" legitimizes the patient as needing help and exempts him or her (for a limited time) from certain responsibilities. It makes clear to the patient that depression is a disorder—that the patient is not to blame and that he or she will recover with appropriate treatment. For example, the therapist might say,

> It's OK if you don't feel like entertaining and being social now, while you're feeling so bad. Why don't you explain directly to your husband that for the next month, during this phase of active treatment for your depression, you would rather not invite guests and would like a chance to consider social obligations with him before he commits both of you to them? You are going to be actively engaged in treatment with me now, and over the next month we will be working hard toward your recovery. The expectation is that you will be able to assume your normal life gradually and at the end of 2 months should be quite active. As time goes on and we begin to understand and cope with the problems around your becoming depressed, we have every reason to hope that you will feel even better than before. (1, p. 84–85)

Table 4–2 lists the major therapeutic tasks for the initial phase of IPT treatment.

Intermediate Phase

After the principal problem area or areas are defined and the treatment contract is agreed on, the intermediate phase of IPT focuses on one of the four principal problem areas. Within each

TABLE 4–2.	Phase I of interpersonal psychotherapy (IPT)—initial sessions

A. Dealing with the depression
   1. Review depressive symptoms.
   2. Give the syndrome a name.
   3. Explain depression and the treatment.
   4. Give the patient the "sick role."
   5. Evaluate the need for medication.
B. Relating depression to interpersonal context
   1. Review current and past interpersonal relationships.
   2. Determine with the patient:
      a. Nature of interaction with significant persons
      b. Mutual expectations and whether these were fulfilled
      c. Satisfying and unsatisfying aspects of relationships
      d. Changes the patient wants in relationships
C. Identifying major problem areas
   1. Determine problem area related to current depression and set treatment goals.
   2. Determine what are the relevant relationship factors and what might change them.
D. Explaining IPT concepts and contract
   1. Outline your understanding of the problem.
   2. Agree on which problem area will be the focus.
   3. Describe procedures and practical aspects of IPT.

Source. Adapted from Klerman GL, Weissman MM, Rounsaville BJ, et al: *Interpersonal Psychotherapy of Depression.* New York, Basic Books, 1984. Copyright © 1984 by Gerald L. Klerman, Myrna M. Weissman, Bruce J. Rounsaville, and Eve S. Chevron. Used with permission of Basic Books, a division of HarperCollins Publishers, Inc.

problem area, there is first a general exploration of the problem and then a focus on the patient's expectations and perceptions, followed by a discussion of other options in handling the issues involved and, finally, efforts at new behaviors.

Grief.   Grieving a loss is a normal part of human experience and usually does not warrant psychological intervention. When people have a delayed, unresolved, or distorted grief reaction (e.g., no dysphoric mood), however, therapy is usually necessary to help deal with the resulting depressive symptoms. Table 4–3 shows the major IPT goals and strategies that are useful in the treatment of abnormal grief.

Interpersonal disputes.   Klerman et al. (1) define an interpersonal dispute as "a situation in which the patient and at least one significant other person have nonreciprocal expectations about their relationship" (1, p. 104), resulting in overt or covert interpersonal conflicts. The IPT therapist does not have any preconceived notions of how best to settle the conflict, but helps guide the patient to discover possibilities for successful resolution. Table 4–4

TABLE 4–3.   **Goals and strategies in the treatment of grief**

A. Goals
  1. Facilitate the mourning process.
  2. Help the patient reestablish interests and relationships to substitute for what has been lost.

B. Strategies
  1. Review depressive symptoms.
  2. Relate symptom onset to death of significant other.
  3. Reconstruct the patient's relationship with the deceased.
  4. Describe the sequence and consequences of events just before, during, and after the death.
  5. Explore associated feelings (negative as well as positive).
  6. Consider possible ways of becoming involved with others.

TABLE 4–4.	**Goals and strategies in the treatment of interpersonal disputes**

A. Goals

   1. Identify dispute.

   2. Choose plan of action.

   3. Modify expectations of faulty communication to bring about a satisfactory resolution.

B. Strategies

   1. Review depressive symptoms.

   2. Relate symptoms' onset to overt or covert dispute with significant other with whom patient is currently involved.

   3. Determine stage of dispute:

      a. Renegotiation (calm down participants to facilitate resolution)

      b. Impasse (increase disharmony in order to reopen negotiation)

      c. Dissolution (assist mourning)

   4. Understand how nonreciprocal role expectations relate to dispute:

      a. What are the issues in the dispute?

      b. What are differences in expectations and values?

      c. What are the options?

      d. What is the likelihood of finding alternatives?

      e. What resources are available to bring about change in the relationship?

   5. Are there parallels in other relationships?

      a. What is the patient gaining?

      b. What unspoken assumptions lie behind the patient's behavior?

   6. How is the dispute perpetuated?

Source.   Reprinted from Klerman GL, Weissman MM, Rounsaville BJ, et al: *Interpersonal Psychotherapy of Depression.* New York, Basic Books, 1984. Copyright © 1984 by Gerald L. Klerman, Myrna M. Weissman, Bruce J. Rounsaville, and Eve S. Chevron. Used with permission of Basic Books, a division of HarperCollins Publishers, Inc.

outlines the goals and strategies available for dealing with role disputes.

Role transitions.   In most social systems, individuals maintain several roles at once (e.g., mother, wife, daughter) and make transitions from one role to another (e.g., single woman to wife to widow). Rapid transitions to new or unfamiliar roles or roles that are experienced as a loss or failure may result in depression. Table 4–5 outlines the IPT goals and strategies that are relevant for helping people cope more effectively with role transitions.

Interpersonal deficits.   Some individuals have inadequate or short-lived relationships because they are deficient in the qualities or skills that facilitate interpersonal connectedness. As a consequence, social isolation is quite common for these people. In comparison with the other three problem areas, individuals with interpersonal deficits are usually lower functioning. Progress may be slow, and in a brief treatment, only beginning inroads may result.

Because such patients often have no meaningful present relationships, the IPT work, of necessity, focuses on past significant relationships, the relationship with the therapist, and evolving, new relationships. For people with problems of this type, the therapist can take a very active, directive, and educative stance—for example, teaching communication skills or role-playing anticipated social situations:

> Since you are thinking about attending your high school reunion, why don't we pretend that you are there. What are some possible things you could say when you first see some of your former classmates?

Table 4–6 lists goals and therapeutic tasks for the IPT treatment of interpersonal deficit problems.

TABLE 4–5.	**Goals and strategies in the treatment of role transitions**

A. Goals

   1. Help the patient to mourn and accept the loss of the old role.

   2. Help the patient to regard the new role as more positive.

   3. Restore self-esteem by developing a sense of mastery regarding demands of new roles.

B. Strategies

   1. Review depressive symptoms.

   2. Relate depressive symptoms to difficulty in coping with some recent life change.

   3. Review positive and negative aspects of old and new roles.

   4. Explore feelings about what is lost.

   5. Explore feelings about the change itself.

   6. Explore opportunities in new role.

   7. Realistically evaluate what is lost.

   8. Encourage appropriate release of affect.

   9. Encourage development of social support system and of new skills called for in new role.

Source.　Reprinted from Klerman GL, Weissman MM, Rounsaville BJ, et al: *Interpersonal Psychotherapy of Depression.* New York, Basic Books, 1984. Copyright © 1984 by Gerald L. Klerman, Myrna M. Weissman, Bruce J. Rounsaville, and Eve S. Chevron. Used with permission of Basic Books, a division of HarperCollins Publishers, Inc.

Termination Phase

In the last phase of IPT treatment, termination should be specifically addressed at least two to four sessions before the contracted end of therapy. This allows time to accomplish the three major tasks of the termination phase:

1. Explicit discussion of the end of treatment

2. Acknowledgment of termination as a time of potential grieving, with the patient being informed that it is common for

TABLE 4–6.	Goals and strategies in the treatment of interpersonal deficits

A. Goals

  1. Reduce the patient's social isolation.

  2. Encourage the formation of new relationships.

B. Strategies

  1. Review depressive symptoms.

  2. Relate depressive symptoms to problems of social isolation or unfulfillment.

  3. Review past significant relationships, including their negative and positive aspects.

  4. Explore repetitive patterns in relationships.

  5. Discuss patient's positive and negative feelings about therapist and seek parallels in other relationships.

Source. Reprinted from Klerman GL, Weissman MM, Rounsaville BJ, et al: *Interpersonal Psychotherapy of Depression.* New York, Basic Books, 1984. Copyright © 1984 by Gerald L. Klerman, Myrna M. Weissman, Bruce J. Rounsaville, and Eve S. Chevron. Used with permission of Basic Books, a division of HarperCollins Publishers, Inc.

patients to be sad, angry, or anxious about ending treatment but that these feelings do not forecast a return of the depression

3. Movement toward the patient's recognition of his or her own competence to deal with problems

With regard to the last task, the therapist, throughout the sessions, should highlight the patient's successes, draw attention to the supports (e.g., friends, church) that exist outside of therapy, and acknowledge the ways in which the patient is beginning to manage more adequately on his or her own.

Sometimes the patients' anxiety about "being on their own" causes them to ask for more sessions or even to regress to previously inadequate levels of coping. The IPT therapist should not be perturbed or dismayed at this understandable occurrence. (See

Chapter 3 on Mann's model for a related view of the termination phase of therapy.) To the patient whose depression has ameliorated but who is still hesitant about ending therapy, the IPT therapist might say the following:

> Many patients have some uneasiness about ending these sessions if they have found them helpful. We have found that a treatment-free period is usually helpful. Let's see how you are doing over the next 8 weeks before making any decisions about further treatment. You can, of course, call me if you need to and treatment will be arranged. (1, p. 141)

If a patient is still severely symptomatic and has shown no progress during the IPT sessions, then the therapist should consider immediately instituting alternative treatments, such as psychopharmacotherapy, a different type of therapy, or IPT with a different therapist.

■ CLINICAL ILLUSTRATION

As an illustration of IPT formulation and technique, the IPT of depressed HIV-positive outpatients is discussed here. This population was chosen because IPT has much to offer in the treatment of chronically ill or medically compromised individuals who develop depressive symptoms, and because there is an urgent public health need to treat patients who are infected with HIV. Markowitz et al. (8) considered that the IPT format and four problem areas were especially relevant for depressed HIV-positive individuals. Specifically, they reasoned that:

1. The individual treatment format (as opposed to group therapy) is more appropriate when concerns about confidentiality are salient.
2. The possibility of flexibility in scheduling was conducive to a physically ill patient who might have many medical appointments or hospitalizations.

3. The engaging, active, and reassuring stance of the IPT therapist, IPT's emphasis on opportunities in the here-and-now, and
   its fostering of interpersonal connectedness and activity might
   counteract the demoralization and passivity that often accompany both depression and medical illness.

In a pilot study, seven overlapping aspects of IPT were found to
be especially helpful in resolving the depression of HIV-positive
individuals (8). These seven aspects are discussed in the sections
that follow.

Psychoeducation About the Sick Role

In the initial phase of treatment, HIV outpatients were told that they
had two medical conditions—depression and HIV infection. They
were informed about the symptoms of depression, such as feelings
of worthlessness and impairments in sleep and appetite. Many of
the patients had attributed these symptoms solely to their HIV
status, which served only to increase their depression. Realization
that some of their problems were due to a treatable psychiatric
condition helped foster hope.

Here-and-Now Framework

IPT's focus on present circumstances helped patients avoid dwell-
ing on "if onlys" with regard to obsessively blaming themselves for
contracting HIV. The therapist emphasized that depression was due
to present problems and therefore solutions could be found.

Interpersonal Formulation

Before treatment, patients thought that depression was an unavoid-
able consequence of their terminal condition. With IPT, they became able to differentiate between normal, sad reactions to bad
news and clinical depression. In fact, studies have found that most
people with incurable illnesses are not clinically depressed (9). The

IPT therapist treating HIV-positive patients may say something like the following:

> Your symptoms are part of depression, and that depression is related to what's been happening in your interpersonal situation. [Examples of difficulties in the patient's present situation are described.] Although your situation feels hopeless and untreatable, it isn't. That feeling is a symptom of depression, a highly treatable and common disorder. About 1 in 10 Americans become depressed sometime in their lifetimes; they nearly always get better with treatment. Depression affects and is affected by interpersonal relationships. [At this point, the therapist identifies social withdrawal, losses, and altered relationships in the patient's life.] Interpersonal therapy, a brief treatment based on this connection, has been proven to be as effective as medication or any other treatment for the kind of depression you have. We'll try to focus on the stresses and relationships in your life that may be contributing to depression. (8, p. 887)

Exploring Options

The depressed HIV-positive patients often had the sense that their lives were already over and they were waiting to die, although most were physically asymptomatic. IPT challenged their perceptions by reframing their illness as an opportunity to assess their present relationships and make changes to correct problems when possible. At the conclusion of IPT, the patients were buoyed by the realization that there are usually always options.

Problem Areas

Although most of the HIV-positive patients had major issues in three or all four of the IPT problem areas (e.g., complicated bereavement, disputes with partners, job loss, social isolation), the IPT therapists focused on one or, at most, two areas in order to provide structure and promote progress.

Grief.   Four common factors that had hindered the patients' ability to deal with grieving before treatment were anticipatory mourning of their own death, survivor guilt over outliving others, fear of rejection by others should they learn of their HIV status, and emotional numbing from encountering so many deaths of friends and loved ones. The IPT therapists addressed each of these impediments to resolving grief. For example, they examined the patients' beliefs that family members could not accept them if they knew their HIV status and/or sexual orientation and suggested that they test their expectations with potentially supportive relatives.

Interpersonal disputes.   IPT therapy focused on helping HIV patients find ways to reconcile differences, obtain alternative sources of support, and end unrewarding relationships. For example, Mr. B, fearing abandonment, was tolerating being taken advantage of financially by his live-in partner. His therapist pointed out that Mr. B seemed more emotionally capable of living alone than he had assumed. The patient proceeded to check out this possibility by having his partner leave for 2 months at a time. Feeling like he had renewed options, Mr. B no longer felt exploited or feared being alone. As a consequence, his depression lifted.

Role transitions.   Although the IPT therapists acknowledged dramatic and difficult role transitions in the patients' lives, they challenged the patients' passivity. The therapists helped patients anticipate how to best deal with physicians, sexual partners, bosses, and others, necessitated by shifting roles (e.g., from being asymptomatic to developing symptoms to having AIDS).

The patients with HIV manifested problems at both ends of the role transition continuum. Some responded to the transition catastrophically. Mr. C, for example, was psychologically incapacitated with his first bout of *Pneumocystis carinii* pneumonia. He thought it "destroyed everything." He withdrew, gave up occupationally, and waited to die. IPT sessions were spent focusing on his remaining options. As a result, Mr. C was able to reconnect with a former lover and to use this partner's emotional support to encourage him to go after a previously avoided but desired career advancement.

Other patients responded to learning that they were HIV positive by minimizing its impact. Mr. D never told anyone about his medical diagnosis, even while taking care of his dying lover. When his lover died, he took no time off work to grieve. He continued with his stressful job as though nothing were the matter. Eventually his denial caused him to become emotionally and physically overtaxed, and he entered IPT to deal with his depression. The IPT therapist focused on pragmatic here-and-now options for dealing with Mr. D's inescapable transition from health to illness. These options, in keeping with the tenets of IPT, focused on interpersonal parameters, such as how to negotiate with his boss to obtain a reduced workload. The patient was able to implement some of these alternatives and to accept responsibility for making his life better.

Interpersonal deficits.   Markowitz et al. (8) chose not to focus on interpersonal deficits in their IPT with HIV-positive patients, not because some of their patients did not have such deficits, but rather because other types of problems would be easier to treat in brief therapy. For example, Ms. E, a schizoid individual, learned that she was HIV positive during a blood drive at work. When she told her strict Catholic parents that she had probably become infected in high school following her one sexual relationship, they were extremely upset. Their negative reaction exacerbated Ms. E's guilt and depression, and a suicidal gesture caused her to come for treatment.

Ms. E's therapist did not address her social isolation but rather focused on her present role transition and her interpersonal dispute with her parents. With support and direct interventions, Ms. E was able to reconcile with her mother. At the conclusion of therapy, Ms. E resumed her typical schizoid existence but was no longer depressed or suicidal.

Therapist Confidence

One reason for the success of brief therapy with this sample of HIV-positive outpatients was because the systematic framework of IPT gave the therapists confidence. Any therapist could feel overwhelmed and hopeless treating depressed people with a terminal disease. Framing issues as interpersonal problems to be addressed in the present provided an active, focused, and organized way to proceed. It encouraged the therapists' hope and thereby made them more engaged with and available to their patients.

Termination

The HIV-positive patients related their perspectives of time running out and the need to make every second count. IPT's short-term focus paralleled the patients' view of time as a precious, evaporating commodity. The patients' urgency to make the most of whatever time was available and their desire to maximize meaning in their lives facilitated their involvement in the therapy.

■ EMPIRICAL FINDINGS

The efficacy of IPT has been established in a number of empirical studies. In the National Institute of Mental Health (NIMH) Treatment of Depression Collaborative Research Program (10), IPT was compared with cognitive-behavioral therapy, imipramine hydrochloride plus clinical management, and placebo plus clinical management. For the most severely depressed individuals, IPT was less helpful than medication but was of significantly more benefit than the placebo condition. (Cognitive-behavioral therapy was not significantly more effective than placebo.) In addition, there was evidence of the specific effectiveness of IPT. Superior recovery rates were found for subjects receiving IPT (alone) and those receiving medication plus clinical management. In a follow-up study of the NIMH study participants (11), however, it was found that patients who had received cognitive-behavioral therapy had lower rates of relapse (defined as major depressive disorder or additional treatment) than did those who had received medication or IPT.

DiMascio et al. (12) found that either medication (amitriptyline) or IPT led to equal overall symptom reduction in patients with nonbipolar depression. In addition, the effects of both treatments together were even more effective because the medication improved the vegetative symptoms and the IPT helped with mood, suicidal ideation, work, and interests. A study of depressed outpatients 1 year after treatment (13) with either IPT or amitriptyline, alone or in combination, found that almost all patients were functioning rather well. However, those who had received IPT (with or without medication) did better with regard to their social functioning.

A pilot study (8) with 23 depressed HIV-positive individuals (most of whom were homosexual or bisexual men) indicated that IPT (with an average length of 16 sessions) was successful in resolving the depression of 87% of the sample. In a later paper, Markowitz et al. (14) presented preliminary data from two treatment modalities of a randomized clinical trial (paralleling that of the NIMH Collaborative Research Program). They found that for depressed HIV-positive patients who were not acutely ill, IPT was more successful than supportive psychotherapy in lessening depression. Differences were observable by the middle of treatment (8 weeks) and remained at termination. Patients receiving IPT benefited with increased functioning physically as well as emotionally. The researchers concluded that therapists should not feel so disheartened about their abilities to help this patient population in short-term therapy.

■ RELEVANCE FOR MANAGED CARE

IPT is quite amenable to the tenets of managed care. The active, directive, and reassuring stance of the therapist and the focus on symptomatology (rather than on personality change or personal growth) in a time-limited treatment are consistent with managed care's philosophy of providing the least intrusive, most cost-effective treatment. Furthermore, IPT has a solid empirical base and a straightforward therapeutic approach, concentrating on here-and-now problems with here-and-now solutions. Finally, the goal of IPT to help patients become as active and interactive in their worlds as quickly as possible is compatible with managed care's emphasis on decreasing dependency on health providers. In this regard, the IPT therapist encourages the patient to find supports outside the therapy so that the process of change is facilitated by relevant, real-world (i.e., nonprofessional and therefore less costly) factors.

■ REFERENCES

1. Klerman GL, Weissman MM, Rounsaville BJ, et al: Interpersonal Psychotherapy of Depression. New York, Basic Books, 1984
2. Fairburn CG, Jones R, Peveler RC, et al: Three psychological treatments for bulimia nervosa. Arch Gen Psychiatry 48:463–469, 1991
3. Klerman GL, Weissman MM (eds): New Applications of Interpersonal Psychotherapy. Washington, DC, American Psychiatric Press, 1993
4. Weissman MM: Mastering Depression: A Patient's Guide to Interpersonal Psychotherapy. Albany, NY, Graywind, 1995
5. Karasu BT: Toward a clinical model of psychotherapy for depression: systematic comparison of three psychotherapies. Am J Psychiatry 147:133–147, 1990
6. Bloom BL: Planned Short-Term Psychotherapy. Boston, MA, Allyn and Bacon, 1992
7. Sotsky SM, Glass DR, Shea MT, et al: Patient predictors of response to psychotherapy and pharmacotherapy: findings in the NIMH Treatment of Depression Collaborative Research Program. Am J Psychiatry 8: 997–1008, 1991
8. Markowitz JC, Klerman GL, Perry SW: Interpersonal psychotherapy of depressed HIV-positive outpatients. Hosp Community Psychiatry 43:885–890, 1992

9. Cella DF, Perry SW: Depression and physical illness, in Phenomenology of Depressive Illness. Edited by Mann JJ. New York, Human Sciences Press, 1988, pp 220–237

10. Elkin I, Shea MT, Watkins JT, et al: National Institute of Mental Health Treatment of Depression Collaborative Research Program: general effectiveness of treatments. Arch Gen Psychiatry 46:971–982, 1989

11. Shea MT, Elkin I, Imber SD, et al: Course of depressive symptoms over follow-up: findings from the National Institute of Mental Health Treatment of Depression Collaborative Research Program. Arch Gen Psychiatry 49:782–787, 1992

12. DiMascio A, Weissman MM, Prusoff BA, et al: Differential symptom reduction by drugs and psychotherapy in acute depression. Arch Gen Psychiatry 36:1450–1456, 1979

13. Weissman MM, Klerman GL, Prusoff BA, et al: Depressed outpatients: results one year after treatment with drugs and/or interpersonal psychotherapy. Arch Gen Psychiatry 38:51–55, 1981

14. Markowitz JC, Klerman GL, Clougherty KF, et al: Individual psychotherapies for depressed HIV-positive patients. Am J Psychiatry 152: 1504–1509, 1995

CONSIDER THIS APPROACH FOR PATIENTS WHO:

- Have rigid, self-defeating personality styles (often indicative of personality disorders)
- Have a history of dysfunctional interpersonal relationships
- Are difficult patients who are off-putting to treating professionals
- Exhibit negativism, dependency, disrespect, or externalization

5

TIME-LIMITED DYNAMIC PSYCHOTHERAPY

Time-limited dynamic psychotherapy (TLDP) is an interpersonal, time-sensitive approach for patients with chronic, pervasive, dysfunctional ways of relating to others. Its goal is to modify the way in which a person relates to himself or herself and others. The focus is not on the reduction of symptoms per se (although such improvements are expected to occur), but rather on changing ingrained patterns of interpersonal relatedness or personality style.

TLDP makes use of the relationship that develops between the therapist and the patient to kindle fundamental changes in the way a person treats others and himself or herself. Its premises and techniques are broadly applicable regardless of time limits. However, its method of formulating and intervening makes it particularly well suited for the so-called difficult patient seen in a brief or time-limited therapy.

Historically, TLDP is rooted in an object-relations framework (1). As such, the search for and maintenance of human relatedness is considered to be a major motivating force within all human beings. This relational view is in sharp contrast to that of classical psychoanalysis, which emphasizes predetermined mental structures to deal with conflicts between gratification of instinctual impulses and societal constraints.

A treatment manual describing TLDP was developed for research purposes and published in book form (*Psychotherapy in a New Key: A Guide to Time-Limited Dynamic Psychotherapy* [2]). A recently published clinical casebook (*Time-Limited Dynamic Psychotherapy: A Guide to Clinical Practice* [3]) translates TLDP principles and strategies into pragmatically useful ways of thinking and intervening for the practitioner.

■ CONCEPTUAL FRAMEWORK

Assumptions

The TLDP model makes five basic assumptions, which are described here.

1. Behaviors learned in the past.   Disturbances in adult interpersonal relatedness usually stem from faulty relationships with early caregivers, most frequently in the parental home. The child learns that he or she must behave in certain ways in order to stay emotionally connected with others (4). These learned behaviors form the building blocks of what will become organized and encoded experiential, affective, and cognitive data (interpersonal schemas) informing one about the nature of human relatedness.

2. Interactive style maintained in the present.   Although one's dysfunctional interactive style is learned early in life, this style must be supported in the person's present adult life for the interpersonal difficulties to continue. For example, if a child has learned to be placating and deferential because he grew up in a home with authoritarian parents, he will unwittingly and inadvertently attempt to maintain this role as an adult by inducing others to act harshly toward him. Thus, dysfunctional interactions, including that of the patient-therapist relationship, tend to be sustained in the present. Accordingly, one can concentrate on the present to alter the patient's dysfunctional interactive style. Focusing in the present allows change to happen more quickly because time is not spent working through childhood conflicts and discovering historical truths.

3. In vivo reenactment in therapy. The patient interacts with the therapist in the same dysfunctional way in which he or she interacts with significant others, trying to enlist the therapist in playing a complementary role. From an interpersonal therapy perspective, this reenactment is an ideal situation because it provides the therapist with the very situation that gets the patient into difficulties in the outside world.

4. Dyadic quality of the therapeutic relationship. By entering into the relationship, the therapist becomes a part of the reenactment of the dysfunctional interpersonal interaction and becomes a participant observer. The therapist cannot help but react to the patient—that is, the therapist inevitably will be pushed and pulled by the patient's dysfunctional style and will respond accordingly. This transactional type of reciprocity and complementarity (interpersonal countertransference) does not indicate a failure on the part of the therapist, but rather represents his or her "role responsiveness" (5) or "interpersonal empathy" (2). The therapist inevitably becomes "hooked" into acting out the corresponding response to the patient's inflexible, maladaptive pattern (6).

5. Chief problematic relationship pattern. The emphasis in TLDP is on discerning what is a patient's most pervasive and problematic style of relating (which may need to incorporate several divergent views of self and other). This is not to say that other relationship patterns may not be important, but rather that focusing on the most frequently troublesome type of interaction should have ramifications for other, less central interpersonal schemas and is pragmatically essential when time is of the essence.

Goals

The TLDP therapist seeks to provide a new experience and a new understanding for the patient.

New experience.[1]   The first and major goal in conducting TLDP is for the patient to have a new experience. *New* is meant in the sense of being different and more functional (i.e., healthier) than the customary, maladaptive pattern to which the person has become accustomed. *Experience* emphasizes the affective-action component of change—behaving differently and having an emotional appreciation of behaving differently. From a TLDP perspective, behaviors are encouraged that signify a new manner of interacting (e.g., one that is more flexible and independent) rather than specific, content-based behaviors (e.g., being able to go to a movie alone).

In TLDP, the therapist determines the type of new experiences that are particularly helpful to a particular patient based on the therapist's formulation of the case. (See "Clinical Illustration," below). The therapist identifies what he or she could say or do (within the therapeutic role) that would most likely subvert the patient's maladaptive interactive style. The therapist's behavior gives the patient the opportunity to disconfirm his or her interpersonal schemas. This in vivo learning is a critical component in the practice of TLDP. The patient has the opportunity to actively try out new behaviors in therapy, to see how he or she feels, and to notice how the therapist responds. This information then informs the patient's interpersonal schemas of what can be expected from self and others.

---

[1]The goal of a new experience presented here and elsewhere in more detail (3) is somewhat of a modification of that originally presented by Strupp and Binder (2).

New understanding. In TLDP, the patient's new understa[nding] usually involves an identification and comprehension of his or h[er] dysfunctional patterns. To facilitate a new understanding, the TLDP therapist can point out repetitive patterns that have originated in experiences with past significant others, with present significant others, and in the here-and-now with the therapist. Therapists' disclosing their own reactions to the patients' behaviors can also be beneficial. Patients begin to recognize how they have similar relationship patterns with different people in their lives, and this new perspective enables them to examine their active role in perpetuating dysfunctional interactions.

The Cyclical Maladaptive Pattern

The TLDP method of formulating a case is through the use of the cyclical maladaptive pattern (CMP) (2). The CMP outlines the idiosyncratic "vicious cycle" of maladaptive interactions a particular patient gets into when he or she relates to others. These cycles or patterns involve inflexible, self-perpetuating behaviors, self-defeating expectations, and negative self-appraisals that lead to dysfunctional and maladaptive interactions with others. The CMP comprises four categories that are used to organize the interpersonal information about the patient (see Table 5–1).

In addition to these four categories, the therapist should also consider his or her reactions to the patient, asking how he or she feels being in the room with this patient and what he or she is pulled to do or not do. The therapist's internal and external responses to the patient provide important sources of information for understanding the patient's lifelong dysfunctional interactive pattern. One's reactions to the patient should make sense given the patient's interpersonal pattern.

A successful TLDP formulation should provide a blueprint for the entire therapy. It describes the nature of the problem, leads to the delineation of the goals, serves as a guide for interventions, enables the therapist to anticipate reenactments within the context

...ghts, feelings, motives, perceptions, and
...nt of an interpersonal nature. For example,
...'t want to have anything to do with me" (thought).
...the promotion" (feeling). "I wish I were the life of
the party ...). "It seemed she was on my side" (perception).
"I start crying when I get angry with my husband" (behavior).

2. **Expectations of others' reactions:** How the patient imagines others will react to him or her in response to some interpersonal behavior (act of the self). "My boss will fire me if I make a mistake." "If I go to the dance, no one will ask me to dance."

3. **Acts of others toward the self:** Actual behaviors of other people, as observed and interpreted by the patient. "When I made a mistake at work, my boss avoided me." "He asked me to dance, but only because he felt sorry for me."

4. **Acts of the self toward the self:** Behaviors or attitudes toward oneself by oneself. "When I disappoint someone, I tend to berate myself." "When no one asked me to dance, I told myself it's because I'm fat, ugly, and unlovable."

---

of the therapeutic interaction, and provides a way to assess whether the therapy is on the right track, in terms of outcome at termination as well as in-session "mini-outcomes." The CMP is a fluid working formulation that is meant to be refined as the therapy proceeds.

■ INCLUSION AND EXCLUSION CRITERIA

Five major selection criteria are used in determining a patient's appropriateness for TLDP:

1. Patients must be in emotional discomfort so that they are motivated to endure the often challenging and painful process of change and to make sacrifices of time, effort, and money as required by therapy.

2. Patients must come for appointments and engage with the therapist, or at least talk. Initially, such an attitude may be fostered by hope or faith in a positive outcome. Later, it might stem from actual experiences of the therapist as a helpful partner.

3. Patients must be willing to consider how their relationships have contributed to distressing symptoms, negative attitudes, and/or behavioral difficulties. Suitable patients do not actually have to walk in the door indicating that they have difficulties in relating to others. Rather, in the give and take of the therapeutic encounter, they must evidence signs of being willing to consider the possibility that they have problems relating to others.

4. Patients need to be willing to examine feelings that may hinder more successful relationships and may foster more dysfunctional ones.

5. Patients should be capable of having a meaningful relationship with the therapist. The patient must have the capacity to experience and relate to others as separate, whole persons so that new interpersonal experiences can be perceived and reenactments of dysfunctional relationships within the therapy can be examined.

The type of patient who is not suitable for TLDP is one who is not able to attend to the process of a verbal give-and-take with the therapist (e.g., a patient with delirium, dementia, or psychosis) or who cannot tolerate the active, interpretative, interactive therapy process, which often heightens anxiety (e.g., a patient who has impulse control problems, abuses alcohol or other drugs, or has a history of repeated suicide attempts).

■ **TREATMENT**

Table 5–2 lists the steps in TLDP intervention. These steps should not be thought of as separate techniques applied in a linear, rigid

---

TABLE 5–2. **Steps in time-limited dynamic psychotherapy formulation and intervention**

---

1. Let the patient tell his or her own story.

2. Explore the interpersonal context of symptoms or problems.

3. Use the categories of the cyclical maladaptive pattern to gather, categorize, and probe for information.

4. Listen for themes in past and present relationships and in the patient's manner of interacting in session.

5. Be aware of reciprocal reactions (countertransferential pushes and pulls).

6. Be vigilant for reenactments of dysfunctional interactions in the therapeutic relationship.

7. Explore the patient's reaction to the evolving relationship with the therapist.

8. Develop a cyclical maladaptive pattern describing the patient's predominant dysfunctional interactions.

9. From the cyclical maladaptive pattern, outline the goals of treatment.

10. Facilitate the experience of adaptive relating with the therapist, consistent with the cyclical maladaptive pattern (goal 1).

11. Help the patient identify and understand the dysfunctional pattern as it occurs in and out of session (goal 2).

12. Help the patient to appreciate the once-adaptive function of the cyclical maladaptive pattern.

13. Revise and refine the cyclical maladaptive pattern throughout therapy.

Source.   Adapted from Levenson H, Shiang J: "Case Formulation in Time-Limited Dynamic Psychotherapy." *In Session: Psychotherapy in Practice* 1:19–34, 1995. Copyright © 1995 John Wiley & Sons. Used with permission of John Wiley & Sons, Inc.

---

fashion, but rather as guidelines for the therapist to be used in a fluid and interactive manner.

In the initial sessions, the therapist lets the patient tell his or her own story (step 1) rather than relying on the traditional psychiatric interview. By listening to how the patient tells his or her story (e.g., deferentially, cautiously, dramatically) as well as to the content of the story, the therapist can learn much about the patient's interpersonal style. The therapist then explores the interpersonal context of the patient's symptoms or problems (step 2) to determine when the problems began and what else was going on in the patient's life at that time, especially of an interpersonal nature. By using the four categories of the CMP and his or her own reactions (step 3), the therapist begins to develop a picture of the patient's idiosyncratic, interpersonal world, including the patient's views of himself or herself and expectations of others' behavior.

The therapist listens for themes in the emerging material by seeing commonalities in the patient's transactional patterns over person, time, and place (step 4). As part of interacting with the patient, the therapist will be pulled into responding in a complementary fashion, recreating a dysfunctional "dance" with the patient. By examining the patterns of the here-and-now interaction and by using the expectations of others' reactions and the behavior of others components of the CMP, the therapist becomes aware of his or her countertransferential responses (steps 5 and 6). The therapist can then help the patient explore his or her reactions to the relationship that is forming with the therapist (step 7). By incorporating all the historical and present interactive thematic information, the therapist can develop a narrative description of the patient's idiosyncratic CMP (step 8).

From this formulation, the therapist then discerns the goals for treatment (step 9). The first goal involves determining the nature of the new experience (step 10). The therapist discerns what he or she could say or do (within the therapeutic role) that would most likely subvert or interrupt the cyclical, dynamic nature of the patient's maladaptive interactive style.

In TLDP, the most potent intervention capable of providing a new understanding (step 11) is thought to be the examination of the here-and-now interactions between the therapist and the patient. It is chiefly through the therapist's observations about the reenactment of the cyclical maladaptive pattern in the sessions that the patient begins to have an in vivo understanding of his or her behaviors and stimulus value. The therapist can help depathologize (step 12) the patient's current behavior and symptoms by helping him or her to understand their historical development. From the TLDP point of view, symptoms and dysfunctional behaviors are the individual's attempt to adapt to situations that threaten interpersonal relatedness. For example, in therapy a passive, anxious client began to understand that as a child he had to be subservient and hypervigilant in order to avoid beatings. This learning enabled him to view his present interpersonal style from a different perspective and allowed him to have some empathy for his childhood plight.

Finally, step 13 involves the continuous refinement of the CMP throughout therapy. In a brief therapy, the therapist cannot wait to have all the "facts" before formulating the case and intervening. As the therapy proceeds, new content and interactional data become available that might strengthen, modify, or negate the working formulation.

■ CLINICAL ILLUSTRATION

As a way of illustrating how the CMP can be a blueprint for therapy, the first 5 minutes of a first meeting between a therapist and a patient is presented. The patient is a 74-year-old man who was about to be discharged from an inpatient psychiatry unit. He had been hospitalized for depression and binge drinking and was now being referred for outpatient treatment.

This clinical vignette can be used by the reader to think about what might be this patient's lifelong dysfunctional interpersonal problem—his CMP. It can be helpful for the reader to be aware of his or her reactions to the patient—the interactive countertransference—and to imagine how interacting with this patient would pull or push a therapist to behave. After thinking about all of this, one can consider what would be the therapeutic goals—specifically, what new experience and new understanding would be desirable for the patient to have in the brief therapy. Finally, the reader may imagine how this man's CMP might be reenacted with the therapist during their sessions.

Therapist: Maybe the best way to get to know you is to have you tell me what brought you into the hospital, what's been going on, and how I can be of help.

Patient [in a whiny, complaining tone]: Well, it started in June. We were living in San Carlos, my daughter and I. We have four children. But Susan, the youngest, lived with me the longest. We just got a notice from the landlord one day that he was going to move into our apartment, and we would have to get out and look for another place. So I started looking. We had a cat, too. I started looking all over San Carlos and, ah, down that whole area. My daughter was working down there. And, ah, we just couldn't find a place at all who would take animals. So they decided somebody has to take care of our cat—a relative. But we still couldn't find a two bedroom apartment for less than $700 or $800. It was just terrible. And, ah, I would go out every day. And go through the listings—the real estate listings. And go look. I got exhausted and got depressed and I started to drink a lot. I just couldn't find anything.

Therapist: When was this?

Patient: Well, we got the notice in June that he wanted us out by July. But then . . .

Therapist: So just last month?

Patient: No, no, no, a year ago.

Therapist: You are talking about a year ago? OK.

Patient: What happened was, I started getting depressed and nervous and exhausted and started drinking. *[Sigh.]* We finally found a place that we could afford, you know, $700, which was way out in Tilton and it was at the end of a dead-end street—way up on a high place. *[Deep sigh.]* It was very isolated. Anyway, I knew something was wrong—I was really behaving weirdly, so I came over here and they started taking me at the Day Treatment Center. I would come here every day to the Day Treatment Center. That was in October. Anyway, I was taking Librium and a sleeping pill *[pause],* but I was still drinking. And I *[deep sigh]* . . . so my daughter complained to Betty, the nurse, down there about it, and Betty had me admitted to the Psychiatry Inpatient Unit. And I was there a couple of weeks. And then they convinced me I should go to the Alcohol Inpatient Unit. So I spent a month in there and I quit drinking. Ah, but I was still depressed. So I came back one day for this depression to the admissions and they admitted me again.

Therapist: Back to the Alcohol Inpatient Unit?

Patient: No, to Psychiatry. And I was there through June. Well, that's about it.

The therapist in this case was feeling irritated, frustrated, disconnected, bored, and guilty for not feeling more positively toward this patient. She was put off by his whiny and passive presentation. Using these countertransferential feelings plus information the patient had provided about his present and past interactions (from the entire session), she derived the following CMP:

The patient is a very isolated, depressed, and dependent man who expects others to know best what he should do. He waits for them to assume responsibility for his life. Others do step in and direct him, perhaps because they feel sorry for him, or because they get worn down by his whiny passivity, or because they feel guilty for not wanting to do more. However, eventually they get frustrated and irritated by his hapless stance and defeatist attitude; they become angry and/or reject him. Although the patient may initially comply with others' directives and demands, he ends up not feeling helped, but rather rejected, unloved, and worthless. Unable to feel effective and nurtured, he feels helpless and hopeless, leading to his increased drinking, isolation, and depression and thereby completing the cycle. A diagram of this patient's CMP is shown in Figure 5–1.

In thinking about what new experiences would help interrupt this maladaptive pattern, the therapist reasoned that if the patient could feel more empowered and more in control of his life—more purposeful, active, and involved—he would be less likely to be so passive and thus less likely to be seen as a whiny complainer by others. The therapist also wanted the patient to have a new under-

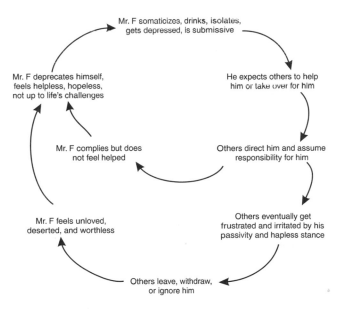

FIGURE 5–1. **Patient's cyclical maladaptive pattern.**

standing that he has capabilities, that he does not need to take a victim stance in life, and that his feelings are important and need not be avoided (by drinking, for example).

An excerpt from the third session illustrates how the TLDP formulation helped the therapist decide how to provide a new experience for the patient. The patient started off by telling the therapist that he had not eaten breakfast that morning.

Patient: I feel pretty low.

Therapist: Do you think it's more than not eating breakfast?

Patient: Well, I don't know.

Therapist: How come you didn't eat breakfast?

Patient: I just hurried over here. I feel nervous.

Therapist: You feel nervous? Why is that?

Patient: I should get some breakfast. I just felt nervous all week, you know. *[Pause.]* I take a stool softener and I had a little accident driving over and I'll have to clean it up, when I get back.

Therapist: Was that upsetting to you?

Patient [sighing]: Yes, it was. It happened before.

Therapist: But that isn't why you've been nervous all week.

Patient: My son's mad at me and all that.

Therapist: Why is your son mad at you?

Patient: For not being friendly with his girlfriend.

Therapist: How do you feel when your son gets mad at you?

Patient: I feel very sad, because we used to get along quite well.

Therapist: So you get sad when he gets mad.

Patient: Yeah. *[Silence.]*

Therapist: Is that pretty typical for you, to get sad when anyone gets mad at you, or just your son?

Patient: I get sad when anyone gets mad at me. My kids are mad at me now because I'm not responding to treatment. I'm not doing anything. I'm just sitting around, so I feel pretty sad.

Therapist: What do they mean you're not responding to treatment?

Patient: They tell me I have to help myself, which is true.

Therapist: You're coming here.

Patient [deep sigh]: Boy, I feel pretty weak.

Therapist: Do you think it would keep you from talking with me—your feeling weak?

Patient: Yeah. I'm having trouble concentrating.

Therapist: And you think it's just because you missed breakfast?

Patient: Because I'm upset about a lot of things. Everything's going wrong. I'm not doing the dishes or helping to take care of the house, and her cat is mad at me because I chase him out of my room when he goes in and sprays.

Therapist: And that makes you sad, that the cat is mad at you.

Patient [half-hearted laugh]: Yeah.

Therapist [in disbelief]: And that makes you sad, that the cat . . . .

Patient: Yeah, I really like the cat.

Therapist: You like the cat. [Yeah.] So the cat's mad at you, and your reaction is to get sad, because the cat is mad at you.

Patient [half-hearted laugh; pause]: There isn't a place in here where I could get a tomato juice or anything?

Therapist: No, not here.

Patient [distressed]: Oh, boy.

Therapist: Mr. F, you are saying two different things. You're saying you would have trouble sitting here continuing with our session because you haven't had breakfast; then you say it's more than that. You would have trouble sitting here talking because you're upset about the things that have gone on this week and it would make this session hard anyway.

Patient: Well, they decided to go up to Oregon to visit some people and they just left and I've been alone for 3 days in the house and I haven't been going out.

Therapist: But right here, sitting here now, do you feel talking with me is difficult because we'll be talking about some upsetting things, or do you think sitting here talking with me is difficult because you didn't have breakfast this morning?

Patient: I think it's because I didn't have breakfast.

At this point, the reader might put himself or herself in the role of the therapist and consider what to say or do. A helpful hint is to remember what the goals of the treatment are. When ready, read on to see what the therapist did to try to create a sense of empowerment on the part of the patient—a sense that he could be the master of his own destiny.

Patient: If I just got something in my stomach I would feel better.

Therapist: Uh-huh. And what keeps you from getting something in your stomach right now?

Patient: I'd have to go over to the restaurant, cafeteria over there. *[Points to next building.]*

Therapist: That's right.

Patient: *[Sigh.]*

Therapist: And what would keep you from deciding to do that?

Patient [sigh]: Well, the fact we're having a session, and I don't want to be rude.

Therapist: So rather than be rude, you'll sit there and be uncomfortable for an hour.

Patient: Well, I don't know. I guess so. Unless you'd let me go.

Therapist: Unless I'd let you go?

Patient [taken aback]: Well, I feel obligated to come and see you, because you're helping me.

Therapist [pause]: Mr. F, I'm not sure what you would like to do right now.

The patient was then put in the position of needing to make a decision. The process of interacting with the therapist around the breakfast issue had raised the saliency of his customary way of denying his own needs in favor of what he thinks others want from him. By making a decision (which provided him with an opportunity to take some action), he was able to experience what it was like to take responsibility for his own behavior. Note that the therapist did not interpret or question the patient's claim that he needed food (e.g., as a resistance), but rather gave him the opportunity to do it differently and see what happened. For example, would the therapist become angry at his assertiveness, as his violent alcoholic father did? (The therapist learned this historical information in a later session.)

■ EMPIRICAL FINDINGS

Although research findings (7, 8) have indicated that therapists can be trained in TLDP, there is some indication that experienced therapists may have an initial decrement in their performance as they grapple with integrating new techniques into their existing therapeutic modes. There is evidence that patients internalize both their own and their therapists' contribution to the therapeutic interaction and that these internalizations are associated with better outcomes (9). In a TLDP research project (10), 71% of patients receiving TLDP for chronic interpersonal problems said they were significantly helped. A long-term follow-up study of these patients indicated that their gains were maintained and slightly bolstered (11). Hartmann and Levenson (12) found that TLDP case formulations convey reliable interpersonal information to clinicians who are otherwise unfamiliar with the case, guide the issues that are discussed in therapy, and lead to better outcomes the more therapists can adhere to them.

■ RELEVANCE FOR MANAGED CARE

Although TLDP is designed to be completed within the 20-session framework of many managed care plans, its focus on changing personality style (or character structure) may seem at variance with managed care's focus on alleviating symptoms. However, TLDP can be a very worthwhile and efficacious approach for difficult patients who do not seem to improve with more symptomatically focused treatments and whose repeated visits to psychiatric and medical professionals result in large expenditures of time and resources. It is certainly an appropriate choice for patients whose chronic interpersonal difficulties cause them to become depressed, anxious, or dysfunctional at work or home.

■ REFERENCES

1. Sullivan HS: The Interpersonal Theory of Psychiatry. New York, WW Norton, 1953
2. Strupp HH, Binder JL: Psychotherapy in a New Key. New York, Basic Books, 1984
3. Levenson H: Time-Limited Dynamic Psychotherapy: A Guide to Clinical Practice. New York, Basic Books, 1995
4. Bowlby J: Attachment and Loss, Vol 2: Separation, Anxiety, and Anger. New York, Basic Books, 1973
5. Sandler J: Countertransference and role-responsiveness. International Review of Psychoanalysis 3:43–47, 1976

6. Kiesler DJ: Therapeutic Metacommunication: Therapist Impact Disclosure as Feedback in Psychotherapy. Palo Alto, CA, Consulting Psychologists Press, 1988

7. Henry WP, Schacht TE, Strupp HH, et al: Effects of training in time-limited dynamic psychotherapy: mediators of therapists' responses to training. J Consult Clin Psychol 61:441–447, 1993

8. Henry WP, Strupp HH, Butler SF, et al: Effects of training in time-limited dynamic psychotherapy: changes in therapist behavior. J Consult Clin Psychol 61:434–440, 1993

9. Harrist RS, Quintana SM, Strupp HH, et al: Internalization of interpersonal process in time-limited dynamic psychotherapy. Psychotherapy 31:49–57, 1994

10. Levenson H, Bein E: VA short-term psychotherapy research project: outcome. Paper presented at the annual meeting of the Society for Psychotherapy Research, Pittsburgh, PA, August 1993

11. Bein E, Levenson H, Overstreet D: Outcome and follow-up data from the VAST project. Paper presented at the annual meeting of the Society for Psychotherapy Research, York, England, June 1994

12. Hartmann K, Levenson H: Case formulation in TLDP. Paper presented at the annual meeting of the Society for Psychotherapy Research, Vancouver, Canada, June 1995

CONSIDER THIS APPROACH FOR PATIENTS WHO:

- Have fairly recently experienced a traumatic or stressful event (As Gaston [1] notes, Horowitz generally does not recommend use of this short-term approach for patients with a complex and long series of linked traumatic events)
- Respond to the traumatic event with intense fear, helplessness, or horror
- Respond to the traumatic event with recurrent and intrusive recollections of the event, distressing dreams, acting or feeling as if the trauma were recurring; and show distress and/or physical activity at exposure to external or internal cues that symbolize the trauma
- Respond to the traumatic event with avoidance of stimuli associated with the trauma or numbing of general responsiveness
- Respond to the traumatic event with marked distress in excess of what would be expected from exposure to a stressor
- Respond to the traumatic event with a decrease in social or occupational functioning

6

SHORT-TERM DYNAMIC THERAPY FOR PATIENTS WITH POSTTRAUMATIC STRESS DISORDER

Mardi Horowitz and his colleagues at the Center of the Study of Neuroses, University of California, San Francisco, have developed a short-term dynamic psychotherapy for dealing with stress response syndromes (2). They developed a 12-session therapy to address posttraumatic stress disorder (PTSD), pathological grief, and other disorders precipitated by recent traumas. Their approach has been used successfully with a wide variety of patients and traumatic situations, including bereaved adults, rape survivors, hysterectomy patients, and combat veterans.

■ THEORY OF CHANGE

Horowitz's approach is based on a specific dynamic theory about how people respond to traumatic events. The theory consists of three components: 1) states of mind, 2) person schemas theory, and 3) control process theory (3, 4). These three components are criti-

Portions of this chapter were modified from Levenson H, Hales RE: "Brief Psychodynamically Informed Therapy for Medically Ill Patients," in *Medical-Psychiatric Practice,* Vol 2. Edited by Stoudemire A, Fogel BS. Washington, DC, American Psychiatric Press, 1993, pp. 3–37. Copyright © 1993, American Psychiatric Press. Used with permission.

cal in understanding the impact of a serious life event such as a trauma. After the occurrence of a trauma, a person is thought to evidence different emotional states and patterns than before the event, referred to by Horowitz as "states of mind." A person may develop a stress response syndrome by responding to the event either with denial and numbing (undermodulation) or with intrusive, repetitive thoughts of the event (overmodulation). Indeed, in many cases, the same patient goes through phases, oscillating between intrusion and denial. This phenomenon underlies Horowitz's position that stress response syndromes are phase oriented.

Person schemas theory holds that the meaning of a life event is not initially integrated into the individual's schemas of self, other, and the world. A serious trauma can fundamentally affect the ways in which people view themselves and their relationships to other people and to the world. For example, the avid jogger who has a heart attack finds that his reaction to the trauma is complicated by the fact that he must change his view of himself as fit and healthy and/or his view of the fairness of the world (e.g., thinking "If I exercise, I am immune from heart attacks").

Control process theory suggests that people use different controls to facilitate or inhibit conscious recognition or communication of conflicts between previous schemas and the new situation brought on by the trauma (5). Previous ideas about the self and the world prior to the event (i.e., schemas that reassure one that the world is a safe and predictable place) are incongruent with the fact that a terrible, traumatic event has taken place. People generally experience this incongruence as very intense, negative feeling states, such as distraught feelings, undesirable thoughts, and anxiety. The individual avoids the agony of these experiences by warding them off.

Each individual has characteristic ways of avoiding or inhibiting these distraught states of mind. In the example of the jogger, the man may find that thinking about his heart attack causes such distress that he avoids thinking or talking about the event. Such avoidance can affect his medical recovery, for example, if he were to avoid doctor appointments or to "forget" to take medications.

The therapist must be sensitive to the meaning of the trauma for the individual. How the patient handles the trauma is further influenced by his or her characteristic modes of warding off undesirable emotional content, which is related to the patient's personality style. The goal of treatment for stress response syndromes is to "reduce the need for controls by helping the patient complete the cycle of ideational and emotional responses to a stress event" (5, p. 170).

■ PATIENT SELECTION

DSM-IV (6) defines PTSD as resulting from exposure to a traumatic event in which the person "experienced, witnessed, or was confronted with an event or events that involved actual or threatened death or serious injury, or a threat to the physical integrity of the self or others" and that "the person's response involved intense fear, helplessness, or horror" (pp. 427–428). Individuals who meet these criteria tend to present with symptoms such as persistent reexperiencing of the traumatic event in dreams, intrusive thoughts, and even actively reliving the experience during flashbacks. Other symptoms include distress in the face of internal or external cues that symbolize or resemble the traumatic event and efforts to avoid thoughts, feelings, conversations, people, places, or activities associated with the trauma. Inability to recall the event, feelings of detachment, hypervigilance, and exaggerated startle response may also be present. In addition to these specific symptoms, more generally observed symptoms may be present, such as restricted range of feelings, difficulty sleeping, irritability and outbursts of anger, and difficulty concentrating.

Another diagnostic group to consider is the adjustment disorders. These diagnoses also require some identifiable psychosocial stressor or stressors to which the patient responds with clinically significant emotional or behavioral symptoms. Generally, the diagnosis of adjustment disorder involves something less than a life-or-death traumatic event (e.g., termination of a romantic relationship or loss of a job). However, the clinician should be aware that an individual's reactions to such events may involve pathological responses that are similar to the reactions typically found under more extreme circumstances. Patients presenting with these symptoms are, in general, suitable for the therapy described by Horowitz and his colleagues.

More specifically, Horowitz's approach is best suited for patients who have experienced a fairly recent traumatic event. The term *fairly recent* is interpreted very generally: Horowitz's approach has been used with adults who have unsuccessfully grieved a loss that occurred some years previously. Childhood traumas with which the patient still struggles may not be appropriate for the 12-session approach, especially if these involved prolonged, repeated traumatization. Use of this brief approach should also not be used with people who have "excessively conflictual or deficient personality structure" (5, p. 168). Exclusions include patients with psychosis or borderline personality disorders, patients involved in litigation, and persons who have experienced a complex, long series of linked traumatic events.

Good premorbid functioning, psychological mindedness, tolerance of pain and interpretations, and the ability to quickly form a good relationship with the therapist are standards in the selection criteria for short-term psychotherapy. It is important to remember, however, that patients who have recently experienced a traumatic event may be exceedingly anxious. Intense, acute anxiety can cause therapists to underestimate a patient's ability to engage in a productive therapeutic process. It is perhaps most useful to consider the patient's history of interpersonal relationships, including the presence of adequate parental figures (1). Patients should not have a long history of psychiatric disturbance, a history of antisocial behavior, a psychotic disorder, or less than average intelligence. Acute suicidality may be observed in people who have recently undergone a severe trauma. By itself, suicidality that can be managed on an outpatient basis does not exclude patients.

These criteria reflect Horowitz's work on a brief, generally 12-session therapy format. Patients with PTSD that involves prolonged childhood physical, sexual, or verbal abuse are unfortunately frequent consumers of mental health services. Sometimes these patients present with evidence of dissociation and even multiple personality. Such presentations are generally not considered suitable for a very brief (e.g., 12-session) treatment course. A time-unlimited format should be considered under these circumstances. In addition, specialized supervision is generally warranted in these difficult cases.

■ GOALS OF TREATMENT

The primary aims of treatment after trauma are to restore functioning and eliminate the symptoms associated with PTSD. With therapy, the overwhelming states of distress and avoidance of thoughts and feelings associated with the event should diminish, along with symptoms like sleep disturbance and irritability. More specifically, however, the patient should be able to diminish the frequency and intensity of both the denial and the intrusive states. Thus, the goal is to achieve a sense of relative mastery over the traumatic event, in which both denial and repetitive reexperiencing are reduced or minimized. One author, Louise Gaston (1), has further specified the main goals of this treatment, as discussed in the following paragraphs.

Acknowledging and Accepting the Traumatized Self

Many patients who have experienced a trauma or loss are seeking relief from their loss of control over themselves and their lives. However, they may deny that they have been affected psychologically. An initial step is for the therapist to help the patient acknowledge and accept the fact that the self has been traumatized and that the reactions are normal and expected in the wake of such a traumatic experience. Some patients judge their own reactions to a trauma as signs of weakness or poor character. The therapist's calm acceptance of the patient's need to cry, complain, or even feel sorry for himself or herself can help the patient take a more sympathetic view of his or her own reactions.

Regaining Mastery

In order to recover, the patient must regain a sense of mastery over both external and internal worlds, within realistic limits. An important aspect of the stress response syndrome is a mistrust of one's self and the world after a traumatic experience. Helping the patient to begin to reenter the world, make decisions, seek support, limit external demands, and control the transitions between intrusions and denial states can help counter the feelings of helplessness associated with loss and trauma.

Integrating the Traumatic Information

The patient must learn to accommodate to the new reality brought about by the traumatic event. Irreversible changes, such as death or disability, may have occurred in the patient's life. The therapist must remember that such accommodations include psychological accommodations but also external, practical considerations. For example, a man whose young wife has just died must make arrangements for child care and other adjustments that are directly the result of the traumatic event. The traumatic event, however, also involves psychological adjustments and changes in the way individuals must relate to themselves and others. This kind of goal involves developing new ways of viewing the self, others, and the world so that a sense of the world as an essentially safe place can be restored.

The attainment of this goal usually ensures that the PTSD symptoms will decrease. For some people, however, such integration is extremely difficult. In these cases, it may be important to lower the therapeutic objective to a partial assimilation of the new information into the person's schemas. Developing new skills around specific tasks that have the effect of restoring functioning, within limits, can be very helpful.

Viewing Trauma as a Challenge

The therapist can help the patient learn to view traumatic events as opportunities for growth. Without being "Pollyanna-ish," the therapist should hold to the idea of at least the possibility that some good can come of a tragedy and that the patient can move forward and have a worthwhile life. Consider the response of the actor Christopher Reeve to his riding accident, which left him paralyzed below the neck. Among other activities, he has begun to lobby for increasing funds for spinal cord injuries. John Walsh, the father of the murdered child Adam Walsh, responded to his grief by changing how law enforcement agencies respond to child abductions. To fully experience life while recognizing its vulnerability and finality is a high-level psychological achievement. To help patients in this regard, the therapist must be comfortable with issues of life, death, and meaning.

These goals will be achieved to varying degrees and in varying sequences by different people. In general, the first two goals, acceptance and mastery, are achieved before integration and viewing trauma as a challenge.

■ TECHNIQUES OF THERAPY FOR PATIENTS WITH STRESS RESPONSE SYNDROMES

Intrusion-Denial Phases

A central aim of the therapist in this form of therapy is to be sensitive to the patient's current phase of response. If the patient is in the intrusive phase, efforts to "get the patient in touch with his or her feelings" may be quite antitherapeutic. For patients who are unable to stop thinking about the event, having nightmares, and feeling flooded with emotion—that is, who are in the intrusive phase—instituting some emotional distance from the event is warranted. This is accomplished with techniques such as providing support, evoking other emotions, and even suppressing emotions. On the other hand, for patients in the denial phase, encouraging feelings is warranted. The overall goal of these techniques is to reduce the amplitude (intensity) and frequency of the intrusion-denial phases and have the patient eventually be able to integrate the meaning of the traumatic event into his or her enduring schemas of life and self. Some of the techniques a therapist can use to deal with the denial-numbing phase and the intrusive-repetitive phase are presented in Table 6–1.

Although mental health professionals are often consulted when a person is in a frightening and overwhelming intrusive phase, sometimes the calmer denial phase is particularly serious when the patient must immediately make important decisions. Dealing with decisions about surgeries or legal matters may be required in the immediate aftermath of a traumatic event. Horowitz (5) has made practical suggestions for how a therapist might deal with time pressure during the denial phase. Intellectualization can be encouraged in discussing with the patient pros and cons of particular decisions. The whole process of intrusion and denial may be described for the patient so that he or she can understand the present state of feeling frozen and unable to concentrate or decide. As a last and temporary resort, the clinician may elicit the support of someone the patient trusts to help make the decisions.

Treating acutely ill patients in the intrusive phase of response. Most of the time, patients seek help for stress response syndromes when they are being overwhelmed with intrusive ideas or emotions. Because of this, Horowitz is quite explicit about how to deal with this response phase. The reality of the traumatic event usually results in a sense of intense need on the part of the patient, to which the therapist wishes to respond swiftly. For physicians, reactions to

TABLE 6–1. Classification of techniques for stress response syndrome

Processes	Denial phase	Intrusive phase
Change Controlling processes	Reduce controls: Interpretation of defenses Hypnosis and suggestion Uncover interpretations	Provide controls: Structure time and events Take over ego functions Reduce external stimuli Rest Permit idealization and dependency
Change Information processing	Encourage abreaction Encourage description: Use images in fantasy Enactments (e.g., role playing)	Remove environmental reminders Differentiate: Reality from fantasy Past self-object images from current ones Suppress thinking (e.g., sedation)
Change Emotional processing	Encourage catharsis Explore emotional aspects Encourage emotional relationships	Support Evoke other emotions Desensitization procedures Relaxation and biofeedback

Source. Reprinted from Levenson H, Hales RE: "Brief Psychodynamically Informed Therapy for Medically Ill Patients," in *Medical-Psychiatric Practice,* Vol 2. Edited by Stoudemire A, Fogel BS. Washington, DC, American Psychiatric Press, 1993, p. 29. Copyright © 1993, American Psychiatric Press. Used with permission. Originally adapted from Horowitz MJ: *Stress Response Syndromes.* New York, Jason Aronson, 1976.

this pressure often result in the immediate prescription of anxiolytics or sedatives. Although this is sometimes warranted, it is also possible that responsiveness by the therapist and establishing a treatment program are sufficient.

The act of talking about the events and having a safe and nonjudgmental place to express one's true reactions to the event can markedly reduce the sense of being overwhelmed. When insomnia results in fatigue and poorer coping capacities, sedation or antianxiety agents may be prescribed on a night-by-night basis. Smaller doses of anxiolytics prescribed for use during the day, again on a dose-by-dose basis, can be used if the patient's anxiety and distress are preventing adaptive functioning (5). Given the potential dangerousness of overdose with such agents, the therapist should remain alert to occult suicidal ideation. Horowitz (5) also warns against the use of antidepressants to relieve immediate sadness and despondent responses to loss. Particularly in the face of a recent trauma, the patient needs to experience and process the natural emotional reactions to traumatic events. These medications are useful, however, if the depressive reaction is pathological and prolonged and meets the necessary diagnostic criteria for major depressive disorder. If psychotherapy alone is not leading to clear, rapid, and progressive improvement, alternative treatments should be considered. However, even if medications are considered appropriate, the working through of the psychological aspects of the traumatic response will be helpful in avoiding relapse once the medications are discontinued.

During the acute phase of therapy with someone who has just experienced a severe trauma, the therapist should be willing to take a very active role. Such work is similar to crisis counseling. More so than in other dynamic therapy approaches, the therapist may directly advise patients to avoid driving, operating machinery, or engaging in tasks for which alertness is essential to safety. Persons already under stress are more likely to have accidents due to lapses in attention, concentration, and sequential planning or because they have startle responses that disrupt motor control (5). Other points made by Horowitz for dealing with the acute phase of treatment include the following:

- The patient remains vulnerable to entering a distraught state of mind even weeks after an event. The effects of experiences such as pangs of searing grief, remorse, terror, or diffuse rage are diminished if the person is surrounded by supportive companions. Persons who have undergone similar traumas (e.g., rape) can be especially helpful, and self-help groups are important resources for such patients.

- The more a person has been traumatized, the longer the phases of response will be. After a major loss, considerable accommodation is necessary in daily life and in one's inner schemas. Getting back to a "normal" pattern of life can take 1–2 years. The therapist should be aware of this and should not push the patient to adjust before he or she is ready. Involvement in productive activities, such as work, are usually helpful in restoring functioning.

- Sleep disruption is a common part of the stress response syndrome. The patient can come to associate relaxation and sleep with feelings of panic and being out of control. This is especially true if the traumatic event happened when the patient felt his or her guard was down. Leaving room lights on, or even having someone sit with the person to "watch over" him or her while he or she is sleeping, may be helpful in this regard.

- The person who has been traumatized may have cognitive impairments of which he or she is not aware. The effects of alcohol may be stronger than would usually be the case. Tactful discussions of these concerns with patients in an acute state are usually warranted.

- The patient's friends and families often gather right after an event, wanting to know what happened. Paradoxically, the need of the patient to talk is likely to come later, when the family and friends may be getting tired of hearing about the event. It is important for the therapist to be able to listen empathically and nonjudgmentally without trying to short-circuit these conversations.

- Many patients expect to be upset immediately after a traumatic event but are surprised and puzzled, even shamed, by responses that come later. They may fear a return of a sense of losing control or have doubts about their recovery. Knowledge of the normal phases of grief, including the fact that intrusive symptoms may occur after a prolonged period of denial, can be very helpful to the patient as a way of normalizing what is going on.

- When evaluating the patient in an acute state, it is important for the clinician to inquire specifically about intrusive experiences. Patients may find these difficult to discuss and worry that they are "going crazy." Here, too, the therapist's communication that these reactions are normal and that more openness about such experiences is helpful rather than harmful can further the therapeutic process.

When the patient does describe the traumatic event, it is important to pay close attention to the details. Sometimes it is important for the therapist and patient to go over and over the experience and the patient's thoughts and fantasies about the events. It is not unusual for the patient to think that he or she did something that caused the event, which then leads to feelings of intense guilt. One young man was referred to therapy by the court for smashing the windows in several parked cars. This patient reported being distressed about the recent death of his brother in a motorcycle accident. It turned out that the motorcycle was the patient's and that he had known that the bike had a faulty plug in the oil pan. He had neglected to tell his brother of this mechanical problem. He believed the oil plug had dropped out, leaking the oil and causing the engine to seize. The seized engine could have caused the bike to go out of control, thereby causing the accident. For this reason, the patient had tortured himself with guilt over causing his brother's death. During one of several "retellings" of the accident, the patient mentioned that he had been the one to pull the motorcycle out of the ditch, start it, and drive it home. The therapist pointed out that had the engine seized, he would not have been able to start the bike and drive it. Although the patient knew about engines, his grief prevented him from recognizing the illogic of his own guilt reaction. Once pointed out in the session, the patient was able to let himself off the hook for his brother's death and begin responding to his grief in a more productive manner.

Treating patients in the denial phase of response. Patients in the denial stage of response, almost by definition, rarely present in overwhelming, acute distress. They may claim to feel down, discouraged, or otherwise dysphoric but do not present with the urgency of patients in the intrusive phase. The danger of this is that unless the therapist is willing to challenge the denial in some way, a collusion between the therapist and the denial can develop. Such collusion threatens to leave the patient with the conclusion that, indeed, the "expert" therapist agrees that nothing is amiss.

To work with patients in the denial phase, it is important to respect the denial, that is, to recognize that the denial is in place for a reason. Someone who has undergone a traumatic event may be terrified of not being in denial. Patients are often quite clear that they see little reason not to be in denial: "Why think about it? Why dwell on what cannot be changed?" Such patients are saying that the only alternative to denial that they can conceive of is an uncomfortable, perhaps uncontrollable, intrusion of feelings.

It is critical for the therapist not to push such patients but to empathize with their need to deny, even explicitly to encourage them to remain on an intellectual level (see "Clinical Illustration" later in this chapter). Horowitz specifies that a major goal with such patients is to help them "dose" the reexperiencing of the event. They can learn that they can remember for a time and put it out of their mind for a time. Control, rather than total denial, is the goal.

Usually patients in the denial phase will discuss an event but do so in a detached way in the third person, as though it were something that happened to someone else. During such periods, asking for details can help the patient move from an intellectualized stance to a more feeling stance. What exactly did they see? What were they wearing? Did they smell anything or hear any sounds? The therapist, however, should not push, but rather should help the patient to organize and express the experience. The therapist should always be mindful of the degree of safety in the therapeutic relationship so that the patient can move into and out of genuine experiencing and processing of the experience.

Content Themes

Although each person has unique ways of responding to trauma because of his or her idiosyncratic history, common themes have been identified in numerous clinical case studies (2). These themes form the basis for the working-through stage of the therapy. Such themes include the following:

- Fear of repetition (real or imagined)
- Shame over helplessness (not being able to stop injury to oneself or to another)
- Rage at the source (including "God")
- Guilt or shame over aggressive impulses (e.g., rageful fantasies toward those who have not suffered the trauma)
- Fear of aggressivity (e.g., a woman who lost a leg feared that she would verbally strike out at other women "showing off" their legs)
- Survivor guilt (e.g., an earthquake victim feels guilty for surviving when others in his building died)
- Fear of identification or merger with victims (e.g., a woman became depressed when her home was spared after a wildfire and her neighbors' homes were destroyed)
- Sadness in relation to loss (e.g., bereavement over the loss of family members in an automobile accident)

Cognizance of these themes can help the therapist in listening to patients and helping them to work through such feelings.

Personality Styles

The value of Horowitz's work is not only in describing the phase-oriented model of treatment, which provides a theoretical framework for directing specific interventions, but also in delineating how such interventions must be modified according to the personality style of the patient. As Horowitz notes, "In brief therapy, the therapist must counter the patient's defensive maneuvers effectively in order to maintain a progressive line of work on the focal problems" (7, p. 44). The interventions the therapist uses must be attuned to these habitual, defensive modes of relating.

For example, patients with a hysterical personality have a vague and diffuse style that keeps them and others from dealing with important conflicts and issues. Patients with more obsessional personalities, on the other hand, may exhibit a ruminating and detail-oriented style that makes them feel in control. Despite this attention to detail, however, the defensive nature of this mode of relating is apparent in the fact that these patients behave indecisively. Horowitz recommends specific therapeutic "counters" to the "defects" in these and other personality styles; that is, to lessen the effects of the stress response, the therapist needs to counter the defensiveness inherent in the patient's style. Table 6–2 lists some of these therapeutic maneuvers for hysterical and obsessional styles. (For a more complete description of the various relationship and intervention maneuvers, see *Stress Response Syndromes* [2] and *Personality Styles and Brief Psychotherapy* [7].)

■ TRANSFERENCE AND COUNTERTRANSFERENCE

Patients who have experienced severe trauma may evidence unique transference reactions in the therapy situation. Some authors (8)

TABLE 6–2. **Some "defects" of hysterical and obsessional styles and their counteractants in therapy**

Style	"Defect"	Counter
Hysterical	Global perceptions	Ask for details
	Impressionistic	Abreaction
	Limited translation of images	Encourage talk
	Misinterpretations	Clarification
	Avoidance of topic	Support
Obsessive	Detailed perceptions	Ask for overall impressions
	Isolation of ideas	Link emotional to ideational meanings
	Misses emotional meaning	Focus on images
	Shifts meanings	Interpretation of defense
	Endless rumination with no decisions	Interpretation of reasons for no decisions

Source. Reprinted from Levenson H, Hales RE: "Brief Psychodynamically Informed Therapy for Medically Ill Patients," in *Medical-Psychiatric Practice,* Vol 2. Edited by Stoudemire A, Fogel BS. Washington, DC, American Psychiatric Press, 1993, p. 32. Copyright © 1993, American Psychiatric Press. Used with permission. Originally adapted from Horowitz MJ: *Stress Response Syndromes.* New York, Jason Aronson, 1976.

have listed a variety of transference reactions that such patients may have to the therapist. The therapist may be perceived as a potential aggressor, a violator of sacred boundaries, an untrustworthy betrayer, an interrogator or judge, a controller, an indifferent witness, and a potential victim of the patient's aggressive impulses. On the other hand, the therapist may be viewed as a caretaker, a friend, a protector, or someone else who might be as lost as the patient feels. An idealizing transference can take the form of viewing the therapist as the possessor of deeper wisdom about life, as someone who can make sense out of the catastrophe and thereby restore the patient's sense of personal meaning (1).

Countertransference reactions are also varied. Four basic ones include 1) becoming hostile toward the patient, 2) feeling over-whelmed or helpless, 3) becoming indifferent, and 4) attempting to save the patient. The therapist's anger can be directed toward the patient because the therapist fears the intensity of the patient's affects or because the experience of the patient's helplessness challenges the therapist's own notions of unalterable control, in-vulnerability, and safety. That is, the therapist may become exas-perated with the patient for not "getting over it," because it is threatening to realize some things cannot be "gotten over." The therapist may overidentify with the patient as a victim, thereby losing the appropriate distance from the patient's experience. This can lead to the therapist taking excessive responsibility for the patient and his or her predicament. In other instances, the therapist may become numb to the overwhelming anxiety and helplessness associated with out-of-control, traumatic events.

It should be emphasized that feelings of anger toward a pa-tient's victimizer or other responsible party are normal reactions on the part of the therapist. However, the therapist must at all times be aware of the potential for vicarious traumatization (1) and take steps (e.g., seek supervision) to ensure that the patient's needs and concerns remain at the forefront of the therapeutic endeavor.

■ CLINICAL ILLUSTRATION

Horowitz (3) describes the case of Ms. G, a young woman who complained of depression because her life was not going well. She wished to examine this problem "conceptually" (3, p. 79). Her main complaint during intake was that she sensed that she was not reacting normally to the recent death of her brother and to her visit home for the funeral. She was preoccupied with this death and the funeral, which led to associative meanings that she was ward-ing off.

In the seventh session, the therapist explored with the patient the meaning of the death as it related to changes in how she viewed her interpersonal world. To get at this material, the therapist asked her consciously to use her often unconscious defense, avoidance of emotion, and intellectual exploration of ideas (recall her stated goal to examine her problems "conceptually").[1]

> *Therapist:* But let's be . . . let's be very rational, very intel-
> lectual about it. What does it really mean to you that
> Sam is dead? *[Pause.]* In terms of you? What does it . . .
> *Patient:* My life?
> *Therapist:* What does . . . what meaning does it have? Be
> very reasonable.
> *Patient:* Well, nothing . . . in terms of the things like com-
> ing in and giving hugs and stuff, it's *[pause]* . . . it
> means the occasional letter that isn't there, the admira-
> tion that he had for me. That asking for big-sisterly
> advice kind of thing *[long pause]*. It means I don't like
> the mention of anything about it *[long pause]*. Um.
> I don't know, doesn't mean, doesn't mean anything
> that I can put my finger on.
> *Therapist:* Yeah, you know, we just took that level and it
> doesn't have any big implications for your life on that
> level at all.

Rather than argue that it does have meaning, which might raise her defenses, the therapist agrees with the patient that it probably does not. This strategy, of going with the defense, often permits patients to become less defensive.

> *Patient:* In a way it does, because it *[pause]* . . . it really
> brings home the unreality of things. And, like, he was
> there on faith. I hadn't seen him for a year, but I knew

---

[1]Transcripted material is reprinted from Horowitz MJ: *States of Mind: Analysis of Change in Psychotherapy.* New York, Plenum Medical Book Company, 1979, pp. 236–246. Used with permission.

he was there. I had the faith. I believed he was there. And now he's not there, and I have to take that on faith, too. *[Sniffles.]* I'm so, uh *[pause],* what's real and what isn't? Is anybody else there? Now, all these people that I remember, that I feel close to, that I have faith in *[pause],* maybe they're not real, either.

In the next vignette, from session 10, the therapist and the patient explore the specifics of her recollections of the funeral and her perceptions of her family. This illustrates how the therapist can help an intellectualizing patient verbalize concerns about the emotional meaning of the trauma.

Therapist: Would you go back in your memory to when you went home after Sam's death and you were with the family? Let's go back to that point in time in your memory. See what thoughts you find in your mind then. Relate it to this issue: They're showing you a lot of grief and you're not showing any, and what should you be doing?

Patient: My mother even said to me that she wished I wouldn't go upstairs and read all the time, but at least I could come down and be with friends. But the implication is that *[mumbles something about that she should be with the family, that this is a time to be together] [pause].* And I felt bad about that but also kind of defiant, and, "Mom, this is what I need to do, and I don't have to be running upstairs all the time with a book and some food" *[pause].* And, um *[pause].*

Therapist: What were you running from? You're not running from reactions to Sam's death at that point. I don't believe that *[pause].* It doesn't hang together well enough. It must be something else, I think.

Patient: You don't think it's because maybe I would have to *[mumbles something about having sad feelings].*

Therapist: Well, maybe. But I don't believe it right now. Let's just . . .

Patient: That's what I thought that it was. That everything I didn't want to deal with . . .

Therapist: I think you didn't want to deal with your family.

Patient: Yeah, I think that's very true *[long pause]*. I didn't want to have to talk with them. I didn't want to have to be comforted by them *[pause]*. I remember crying one night, a night or two after I came home, getting really mad at my mother and going upstairs and starting to cry out of anger and then using the already crying to try to cry about Sam a little bit and feeling better.

Still later, they discuss her perceptions of crying for her brother.

Therapist: You liked the idea of yourself crying [at the funeral]. You clearly felt guilt that you weren't crying.

Patient: M-hm.

Therapist: Whenever you could cry about something, you'd have liked it to be seen by the people.

Patient: Well *[pause]*, definitely I felt it that time, and I was really glad that everybody saw it.

Therapist: You were feeling badly about the way you were, which was angry and disgusted and withdrawn.

Patient: M-hm.

Therapist: And you were also feeling anxious about being sucked in somehow. I mean I think there must have been some anxiety that you would . . . just fold yourself up in her [mother's] arms.

Patient [long pause]: And I kept being tempted to do that, too. Um, came off the plane with my lip-trembling kind of thing and at various times I could have *[pause]* fallen on her breast with tears and wailed. I am definitely afraid of drama because I know I like it, and it's just that it, it's not . . . *[trails off].*

Therapist: Well, this isn't the time in your life to go back to your mother's bosom.

Patient: M-hm. But I, I could have just gotten a little amount of approval *[pause]* by breaking down and crying at certain points but I didn't. Or by not being silly.

Therapist: Mm. No, I think you were feeling maybe unconsciously, that that's kind of dangerous, being sucked in.

Patient: Like, I went out of my way not to.

Therapist: You went out of your way, yeah.

Patient: That really makes sense because I can see her just wanting me to stay there, you know, not go back to California. "Stay here, we need you now."

These vignettes illustrate ways in which the therapist can help the patient begin to identify and work through the feelings associated with a traumatic event.

■ EMPIRICAL FINDINGS

Horowitz's model of therapy has been tested empirically. One early study (9) involved 52 cases of pathological grief reaction after the death of a family member. Using the 12-session format, the authors found significant improvement in all symptomatic outcome variables, as well as positive changes in interpersonal functioning and capacity for intimacy. A randomized clinical trial (10) was conducted for patients with PTSD using three therapy modalities—Horowitz's approach, trauma desensitization, and hypnotherapy and a waiting-list control group. Results indicated that after 4 months, treated subjects presented significantly fewer symptoms related to trauma than did the untreated control group. As is often the case in psychotherapy research, there were no significant differences among the three treatment modalities, although trauma desensitization and hypnotherapy had a greater impact on intrusive symptoms, whereas Horowitz's approach had a stronger influence on avoidance symptoms. These authors pointed out that not all treated patients got better, and they concluded that some combination of Horowitz's dynamic therapy and hypnotherapy may be beneficial to traumatized individuals. They also noted that longer treatments may be more beneficial for such patients.

■ RELEVANCE FOR MANAGED CARE

Horowitz's time frame of 12 sessions is more in keeping with the limits imposed by managed care than many other brief versions of dynamic psychotherapy. Some reviewers for managed care companies may be concerned about covering the diagnosis of PTSD. Such a diagnosis can conjure the specter of extremely disturbed individuals who have suffered lengthy, childhood abuse requiring perhaps years of therapy. This chapter outlines an approach to therapy that is suitable for patients with PTSD in response to a relatively recent and circumscribed traumatic event. As such, it is reasonable that perhaps 12–15 sessions could result in very positive outcomes.

It is important when dealing with managed care reviewers to carefully make the case for the treatment, when appropriate, by outlining how one will specifically target the relevant phasic symptom clusters of intrusion and denial. As with other forms of dynamic therapy in a managed care environment, it is best to deal frankly with limitations of coverage in the therapy sessions, treating such limitations as factors that need to be considered when planning the treatment approach.

■ REFERENCES

1. Gaston L: Dynamic therapy for post-traumatic stress disorder, in Dynamic Therapies for Psychiatric Disorders (Axis I). Edited by Barber JP, Crits-Christoph P. New York, Basic Books, 1995, pp 161–192

2. Horowitz MJ: Stress Response Syndromes. New York, Jason Aronson, 1976

3. Horowitz MJ: States of Mind: Configurational Analysis of Individual Psychology, 2nd Edition. New York, Plenum, 1987

4. Horowitz MJ: Introduction to Psychodynamics: A New Synthesis. New York, Basic Books, 1988

5. Horowitz MJ: Short-term dynamic therapy of stress response syndromes, in Handbook of Short-Term Dynamic Psychotherapy. Edited by Crits-Christoph P, Barber JP. New York, Basic Books, 1991, pp 166–198

6. American Psychiatric Association: Diagnostic and Statistical Manual of Mental Disorders, 4th Edition. Washington, DC, American Psychiatric Association, 1994

7. Horowitz MJ, Marmar C, Krupnick J, et al: Personality Styles and Brief Psychotherapy. New York, Basic Books, 1984

8. McCann IL, Pearlman LA: Psychological Trauma and the Adult Survivor: Theory, Therapy, and Transformation. New York, Brunner/Mazel, 1990

9. Horowitz MJ, Krupnick J, Kaltreider N, et al: Initial psychological response to parental death. Arch Gen Psychiatry 38:316–323, 1981

10. Brom D, Kleber RJ, Defares PB: Brief psychotherapy for post-traumatic stress disorder. J Consult Clin Psychol 57:607–612, 1989

CONSIDER THIS APPROACH FOR PATIENTS WHO:

- Have serious psychopathology in addition to alcohol or drug abuse/dependence
- Are not acutely in need of detoxification or hospitalization
- Have a reasonable degree of stability with respect to their addiction (need not be totally abstinent)
- Do not exhibit signs and symptoms of dementia or other irreversible organic brain syndrome or other medical condition that can create marked changes in mental status
- Are not schizophrenic and do not have another psychotic disorder or untreated bipolar disorder
- Wish to engage in psychotherapy (seek self-understanding)

7

BRIEF DYNAMIC PSYCHOTHERAPY FOR PATIENTS WITH SUBSTANCE ABUSE DISORDERS

Substance abuse disorders present some uniquely difficult issues for dynamic therapy in general and brief dynamic therapy in particular. Indeed, most modern brief dynamic therapies specifically exclude patients who are addicted to alcohol or other drugs (1, 2). Even very strong advocates of brief therapy (3) caution the therapist providing brief therapy to be aware of the possible presence of drug addiction or alcoholism in patients, pointing out the negative effects of substance abuse on brief therapy. Furthermore, psychodynamic psychotherapy and its progenitor, psychoanalysis, have been stereotyped by some authors (4) as "a waste of time" for alcoholic patients, whereas others have noted beneficial effects of psychotherapy on substance-abusing populations (5, 6). Emerging from this confusing picture are several recent efforts to develop dynamic approaches to treat alcoholism (7), drug (especially opiate) abuse (8), and cocaine abuse (9, 10). In this chapter, we draw primarily on the work of Mark and Faude (9) and Mark and Luborsky (10) with persons addicted to cocaine to present some general guidelines for using dynamic therapy with substance abusers.

■ CONCEPTUALIZING SUBSTANCE ABUSE AS A PSYCHIATRIC DISORDER

Substance abuse is a complex disorder that is best conceptualized from a biopsychosocial perspective. This means that there are various known contributors to the disorder, all of which have a real impact on the addiction. The "bio" component refers to the pharmacology of the drug that plays a part in addiction, as do apparent genetic predispositions. The "psycho" component refers to personality factors that are repeatedly observed in substance abusers. These include basic deficits in object relations, chronic interpersonal problems, self-concept deficits, and frequent inability to regulate emotions. The "social" component refers to the complex role that alcohol and other drugs play in our social relations.

Environmental factors, such as home disruptions, disadvantaged upbringing, or history of parental substance abuse and/or mental illness, have been shown to be strongly related to addiction. Social skill deficits (e.g., social and work skills), too, have been shown to be important contributors to substance abuse.

Addiction is unlike other psychiatric disorders in significant ways. Probably foremost among these is that addiction involves a primary urge. This urge—the urge to use—can take precedence over relationships, money, food, and shelter. Often what is striking about the addicted person is his or her inability to stop using despite the loss of family, job, social standing, license to drive, and other basic factors of life.

It should never be forgotten that, at bottom, the person who is truly addicted wants to use his or her drug or to drink, though without the negative consequences of use. That addiction is often "ego syntonic" explains why it is fundamentally unlike some other psychiatric disorders. For example, depressed patients do not want to be depressed. Anxious patients desire nothing more than being rid of their anxiety. Rather than being self-referred to get rid of unwanted symptoms, addicted persons are often in treatment because someone else (a spouse, employer, or judge) has directed them into treatment. In this, substance abuse is similar to some eating disorders and personality disorders.

Within this complexity, psychotherapy can and should play a role. Unlike the approaches to some other problems outlined in this book, the treatment of addictions is much more likely to involve other interventions. These might include family therapy; medication (such as methadone, disulfiram, naltrexone, mood stabilizers, and antidepressants); and Alcoholics Anonymous (AA), Narcotics Anonymous (NA), Cocaine Anonymous (CA), or other support groups. It can be very difficult to treat the severely addicted person with psychotherapy alone (11). This should probably not even be attempted by the novice therapist, who runs the risk of colluding with the patient's wish that his or her problems will somehow "go away" and he or she will not "really" need to stop using. Thus, it is important for the psychotherapist to be knowledgeable about and open to other providers and other approaches to the treatment of addictions.

This discussion of the biopsychosocial conceptualization of addiction raises an interesting distinction for the psychotherapist: Is the psychotherapy directed to the substance abuse or dependence directly, or to comorbid psychiatric problems such as depression and anxiety? There is considerable empirical evidence that patients with a primary diagnosis of substance abuse and a comorbid psychiatric diagnosis benefit from psychotherapy, especially with regard to improvements in their mental health. The evidence for a direct effect on the drug use itself is much less clear. For instance, there is some evidence of the effectiveness of therapy on drug abuse for persons addicted to opiates maintained on methadone (6), whereas psychotherapy has yielded much less of an effect on cocaine abuse (12).

The approach advocated in this chapter is that dynamic psychotherapy should be considered as part of an overall treatment plan that includes some kind of drug counseling and possibly other interventions as well, such as medications and family therapy. Following Mark and Faude (9), we believe that, for some patients, it is "useful to understand the phenomenon of drug [or alcohol] addiction, whatever the causes, in the context of a person's life, including an understanding of the person's personality or character structure" (p. 296). For this, dynamic therapy is uniquely suited.

■ PATIENT SELECTION

The selection criteria at the beginning of this chapter are presented with the understanding that they are relatively broad. There is little in the literature definitively indicating which addicted patients respond to psychotherapy. There are data suggesting that a diagnosis of antisocial personality is negatively associated with outcome. However, even this apparently straightforward exclusion can be misleading, because data also suggest that antisocial patients who are depressed tend to respond positively to dynamic psychotherapy (12). In general, patients who desire psychotherapy and who seek to understand the self-defeating attitudes and behaviors that have contributed to their current situation are most likely to benefit from dynamic therapy. Patients who struggle with sobriety often wish to discuss issues such as personal insecurities, chronic interpersonal failures, or episodes of childhood or spousal abuse. Such problems are not generally dealt with in 12-step (AA, NA) or other traditional approaches that focus on sobriety.

■ THERAPIST'S ATTITUDE TOWARD PATIENTS WITH SUBSTANCE ABUSE DISORDERS

For any therapist who intends to treat patients with substance abuse disorders, a careful self-examination is essential with regard to his or her attitudes toward addicted persons and substance use. The therapist's personal experiences with family members who may use alcohol or other drugs to excess, as well as his or her personal attitudes about drinking and drug use, should be recognized and should not be permitted to interfere with the therapist's reactions to the patient's statements and needs. Most important, perhaps, is for the therapist to see the patient as a *person* who abuses substances, rather than simply as an "alcoholic" or a "drug addict." Viewing the patient as a person with a problem rather than as belonging to a stigmatized category allows the therapist to be more responsive to the entire person and thus able to take a more flexible and understanding approach to the patient. This attitude is arguably the most important therapeutic act and is the foundation for establishing a therapeutic alliance. It has been repeatedly demonstrated that the strongest correlate of positive outcome for substance abusers is the therapeutic alliance (6, 9).

■ TWELVE-STEP PROGRAMS AND GROUP COUNSELING

As mentioned above, the substance abusing patient in treatment is usually involved in treatments in addition to psychotherapy. Most therapists who work with these patients acknowledge a role for the patient's involvement in self-help or support groups. Any therapist who treats people who abuse substances will certainly meet patients who have had much experience with AA or NA, and thus the therapist should have a working knowledge of 12-step programs. It is advisable for therapists who work with substance-abusing patients to attend a 12-step program. Typically, 12-step programs are open meetings that anyone can attend, and attending one personally is a useful experience.

AA, NA, or group counseling directed toward sobriety provide several indispensable services for addicted patients. Group counseling such as that found in intensive outpatient programs can serve to educate the patient about substances and their effects on the body, the mind, and social interactions; can provide a setting for experiencing hope by seeing other addicted individuals beginning the recovery process; and can help lessen the shame of drug and alcohol addiction by allowing the individual to be supported by others who have had similar experiences. Groups such as AA or NA also offer alternative social activities and friends for people whose previous social contacts may be primarily geared toward drinking or using drugs. Particularly, participation in AA or NA affords the patient the opportunity of help at all hours to avoid engaging in substance abuse or other self-destructive behavior during times of crisis.

To understand patients who are in recovery or are struggling with sobriety, therapists working with this population should be familiar with the 12 steps (Table 7–1). These refer to a program for recovery from alcoholism developed by "Dr. Bob and Bill W.," the cofounders of AA. The AA approach and the 12 steps have been very successful in helping countless addicted persons achieve and maintain sobriety. It must also be stated, however, that there are individuals who respond poorly to some aspects of the 12 steps. Statements about personal powerlessness are problematic for some people. Others find the strong references to spirituality in the 12 steps difficult to reconcile with their own personal views on such matters. A referral to Rational Recovery (13) or a drug counseling group may be indicated for these individuals. The important point is for the therapist to recognize that addicted patients need more support and more structure for their lives than is available through individual psychotherapy alone.

■ ROLE OF VARIOUS PSYCHOACTIVE SUBSTANCES

Treatment programs and approaches are often differentiated on the basis of the patient's substance of choice. Thus, there are programs for the treatment of alcohol abuse and for other drug abuse. Despite a similar approach, AA is often differentiated from NA on the basis of the "kind" of individual who attends; for instance, in some places older people with more traditional values tend to participate in AA, whereas younger people with more counterculture values might attend NA. In general, addiction is addiction, regardless of the particular substance used. Furthermore, many substance abusers use multiple drugs as well as alcohol. The common denomina-

TABLE 7–1.   **The 12 steps of Alcoholics Anonymous**

1. We admitted we were powerless over alcohol—that our lives had become unmanageable.

2. Came to believe that a Power greater than ourselves could restore us to sanity.

3. Made a decision to turn our will and our lives over to the care of God, *as we understood Him.*

4. Made a searching and fearless moral inventory of ourselves.

5. Admitted to God, to ourselves, and to another human being the exact nature of our wrongs.

6. Were entirely ready to have God remove all these defects of character.

7. Humbly asked Him to remove our shortcomings.

8. Made a list of all persons we had harmed, and became willing to make amends to them all.

9. Made direct amends to such people wherever possible, except when to do so would injure them or others.

10. Continued to take personal inventory, and when we were wrong promptly admitted it.

11. Sought through prayer and meditation to improve our conscious contact with God *as we understood Him,* praying only for knowledge of His will for us and the power to carry that out.

12. Having had a spiritual awakening as the result of these steps, we tried to carry this message to alcoholics, and to practice these principles in all our affairs.

Source. The Twelve Steps are reprinted with permission of Alcoholics Anonymous World Services, Inc. Permission to reprint the Twelve Steps does not mean that AA has reviewed or approved the contents of this publication, nor that AA agrees with the views expressed herein. AA is a program of recovery from alcoholism *only*—use of the Twelve Steps in connection with programs and activities that are patterned after AA, but that address other problems, or in any non-AA context, does not imply otherwise.

tor is that an individual is experiencing the consequences of abusing a substance and does not seem able to discontinue using. Despite recognition of this basic aspect of addiction, a somewhat artificial distinction persists between alcohol addiction and drug addiction. There are even different branches of the National Institutes of Health that deal with addiction (the National Institute on Alcohol Abuse and Alcoholism [NIAAA] and the National Institute on Drug Abuse [NIDA]). The question for the therapist is, what important differences are there, if any, among addicted persons who primarily abuse different substances?

Our experience is that the primary substance of abuse makes a difference in some treatment decisions but not in others. That is, certain aspects of some abused substances have important implications for treatment. Most notably, perhaps, is that there are medications available for helping patients who are addicted to some substances but not for others. Methadone, for instance, can help the person addicted to opiates control drug cravings, and disulfiram provides the person with alcoholism an incentive not to drink. At present, there are no widely accepted medical interventions for cocaine or crack abuse.

Other differences relate to the legality or illegality of the substance being abused. A number of legal substances can produce addiction. Alcohol, for instance, can be used legally by adults age 21 and older. Addiction to legal prescription drugs sometimes involves illegal methods of procuring the drug. However, some patients, typically those with chronic pain, are legally prescribed powerful painkillers to which they have become addicted. Many of these patients are middle-class, older individuals who resist the idea that they are addicted like the stereotypical youthful criminal or "junkie." On the other hand, of course, are individuals who abuse illegal substances. Issues facing these patients include the fact that mere possession of such substances is illegal and admission of any use can affect a person's job, standing in the community, or even personal liberty.

Many substance abusers are polydrug abusers; that is, they use different chemicals for different reasons. Some individuals may use cocaine or crack to achieve a stimulant effect and opiates or alcohol to become sedated or to sleep. There is also the phenomenon of cutting down or eliminating one substance, such as drug use, and increasing the use of another, such as alcohol.

For the psychotherapist, the issue is not the substance of abuse but the effects of the abused substance on the individual's social and psychological functioning. Thus, confronting addiction means that the patient must face the social and psychological effects (10) of abusing substances, such as

Grief resulting from lost time, lost opportunities, or lost experiences while high
- Muddled or destroyed relationships
- Areas of incompetence that result from having substituted drugs for solving life's challenges
- Fear of approaching those challenges without drugs or alcohol and without the developed techniques for handling those challenges
- The overconfidence that is often used to compensate for damaged self-esteem

These issues may pertain to any addicted person who has been using for a number of years. Often starting during adolescence or in early adulthood, the addicted person in treatment must face the fact that he or she is behind nonaddicted peers in developing relationships, careers, and other areas of life. When the addiction develops in later years, the addicted person must face the loss of what was built earlier in life, such as a marriage or a promising career ruined by an addiction. Even without predominant psychopathology, addicted persons in early recovery generally have to begin dealing with such issues, whatever the primary substance of abuse.

■ SUPPORTIVE-EXPRESSIVE THERAPY FOR COCAINE ABUSE

For the purposes of this volume, we have chosen to describe supportive-expressive therapy of cocaine abuse developed by Mark and Faude (9) and Mark and Luborsky (10). This approach is based on the concepts and techniques of supportive-expressive therapy developed by Luborsky (14). The approach is manualized (10), and its clinical effectiveness for treating cocaine abuse is currently being tested in an NIDA-funded, multisite clinical trial. As discussed above, it is our contention that this general approach should have relevance in the treatment of anyone whose life has been significantly disrupted by abuse of psychoactive substances.

Core Conflictual Relationship Theme

For this approach, it is important to have an understanding of Luborsky's core conflictual relationship theme (CCRT) framework for understanding a person's personality or character structure. Briefly, the CCRT comprises two kinds of responses: the core response from others (RO) and the core response of self (RS). The RO refers to the person's predominant expectations or experiences of others' internal and external reactions to them. The RO could include the other person's actual responses to the patient, the patient's anticipations of others' responses, and the patient's fantasies of others' responses. The RS refers to the patient's own somatic experiences, affects, actions, cognitive style, self-esteem, and self-representations. A third component of the CCRT reflects what the patient desires or yearns for, namely, the patient's "wish." By definition, the wish includes an RS and an RO. These components are usually, though not invariably, interpersonal in nature. Thus, the core RS for Mr. H (whose case is discussed later in this chapter) includes his sense that he is incompetent, foolish interpersonally, and unlikable. His core RO includes the statements "Others don't like me," "Others exploit me," and "Others ridicule me." His core wish is to be loved, admired, and appreciated. Thus, he yearns for others to admire him and to be a grateful audience (wishful RO), whereas his wishful RS is to be the young boy of great promise and talent.

The core RO component for cocaine abusers (and probably for other addicted persons as well) is that they typically expect or experience a range of negative responses from others. These include being criticized, rejected, misunderstood, controlled, and/or humiliated. The core RO component can reflect experiences before or during the substance abuse. In the context of these painful reactions of others, substance abusers may seek solace in a relationship with a drug that seems a more reliable companion and friend than other people. These ROs tend to be associated with the core RS component such as shame, guilt, helplessness, and despair, as well as a sense of victimization that leads to feelings of entitlement, rage, and distrust. The interactions of such ROs and RSs can result in (or result from) great difficulty in identifying, tolerating, and modulating and/or expressing one's emotional experiences. The resulting pain is experienced as overwhelming. In a sense, the drug sometimes serves as a kind of "medication" for dulling the pain of these interactions (or lack of significant interactions) with others.

The wish component for substance abusers sometimes takes the form of the wish to continue using without suffering the consequences. At a deeper level, the substance abuser wishes to have his or her wishes—to be understood, loved, and appreciated—without having to give up the substance. In this way, the addicted person avoids any risk of further pain or disappointment or of having to face the necessary, if not glamorous, responsibilities inherent in a mature, satisfactory life (e.g., taking responsibility for negative self-actions; considering others' needs; responsibly attending to work, school, and daily role activities). Table 7–2 presents some questions for the therapist to keep in mind when interviewing patients because they are useful in organizing the CCRT for an individual patient.

Treatment Goals

Beginning Phase

The first goal of psychotherapy is to establish what has been called a "collaborative relationship" or "therapeutic alliance" with the addicted patient. However, the therapist should never self-consciously

TABLE 7–2.	**Questions for organizing a core conflictual relationship theme**

Wish:

What is the patient's central wish? What gives life meaning for this person? What does the patient want from other people?[a]

Central response from others:

What has the patient come to expect from others? Frequently anticipated negative responses include

- "They don't trust me; they don't believe me."
- "They don't respect me; they are disgusted by me."
- "They treat me in a rigid, authoritarian manner."

Such anticipated responses often are used to justify patients' actions and their response from self. These constitute the patient's *central response from others.*

Central response from self:

How does the patient respond to the frustration of failing to realize his or her basic wishes, and how does he or she act 1) to impede the realization of those basic wishes and 2) to perpetuate the very negative reactions from others he or she has come to anticipate? When these responses fall into a pattern, they are called the patient's *central response from self.*

---

[a] As a patient becomes increasingly dependent on an addictive substance like cocaine, the most basic wishes become increasingly displaced and difficult to recognize. Desires or needs become determined almost entirely by the physiological, psychological, and social effects of the drug.
Source. Adapted from Mark D, Luborsky L: *A Manual for the Use of Supportive-Expressive Psychotherapy in the Treatment of Cocaine Abuse.* Unpublished manual, Department of Psychiatry, Hospital of the University of Pennsylvania, 1992; and from Luborsky L: *Principles of Psychoanalytic Psychotherapy: A Manual for Supportive Expressive Treatment.* New York, Basic Books, 1984.

set out to achieve such an alliance. The patient will most certainly experience this as artificial or manipulative. Patients in general, and perhaps addicted patients in particular, are extraordinarily sensitive to phoniness. Rather, the therapist should focus efforts on 1) instilling a sense of curiosity in the patient regarding his or her psychological functioning, 2) encouraging a sense of hope in the patient, and 3) establishing a sense of purpose and relevance of the therapy sessions early in the therapy.

The first step is to inquire about the patient's goals and central concerns at the beginning of treatment. The patient, however, is liable to come up with goals about which the therapist can do little directly, stating, for example, "I need a job," "I need a place to live away from my mother," or "I need someone to talk to." The therapist must work to frame the patient's goals into terms that can be addressed within psychotherapy. Follow-up questions to concerns such as those just mentioned might be: "What keeps you from getting a job?" "What seems to get in the way of finding a place away from your mother?" or "Why is there no one in your life to talk with?" In each of these or similar follow-up questions, the therapist must search for patients' descriptions of problematic interactions with people that can be used to begin developing a CCRT. In this way, goal setting and developing a CCRT become parallel tasks.

In addition to goal setting, the therapist must attend to other issues with patients who abuse substances, including the following:

- Patient attendance at sessions is often poor, sometimes because they are using. The shame experienced by patients after having used can compound the already powerful reluctance to engage in treatment. For this reason, it is unwise for the therapist to adopt the traditional, passive role. The therapist should, in most cases, call the patient after a missed session rather than waiting for the patient to contact the therapist.
- The therapist should avoid being rigid and should not adopt an anonymous, "neutral" analyst role. The traditional passivity of the dynamic therapist tends to be less effective with substance abusers than adopting a warm, flexible, and natural therapeutic attitude.

- When discussing abstinence, the therapist should avoid engaging in arguments or generating an adversarial position by insisting on abstinence. Although the therapist should recommend abstinence from all psychoactive substances, some patients contend that they can control their use or can use another substance (e.g., a person addicted to cocaine might insist that drinking is not a problem). One approach might be to take a "let's see" attitude by proposing an experiment in which the patient is asked to abstain from any drugs for a mutually agreed on amount of time.
- The therapist should help patients to experience and express how vital they feel drugs are to their lives.
- Finally, the therapist should advise the patient to attend a 12-step meeting. Early in treatment, the goal is to get the patient to try out self-help programs and find a 12-step group with which they are comfortable. There are great differences among these groups, and in any reasonably sized town, there should be several regular meetings from which to choose. The therapist should encourage the patient to try several to find one that he or she likes.

Middle Phase

The central goal for the middle phase of treatment is to frame the patient's goals into a CCRT framework and to proceed to work on it. Specifically, the therapist should attempt to tie the components of the substance use into the following content areas:

- The meaning, functions, and consequences of the substance use should be explored. Thus, the therapist should look for how wishes, ROs, and RSs contribute to the patient's incidents of substance abuse. For example, a patient described using after his ex-wife refused to let him see his children. In this example, the therapist explored with the patient his primary wish, anticipation of others' (e.g., ex-wife's) responses, and his response from self (e.g., driving to his contact, purchasing and using the drug, missing work the next day).

- The CCRT is used to illuminate roadblocks encountered during the patient's attempts to become drug free. Even when the patient sincerely wants to stop using, the process is never as simple as "Just say no." For example, a person who denigrates himself and others will have great difficulty in getting help from an AA sponsor, group members, even the therapist. The therapist should explore how the patient's anticipated responses from others and the response from himself or herself get in the way of achieving the patient's own goal of a drug-free life.

- The patient's difficulties in living without drugs are framed within the CCRT. For example, making new friends, adjusting to a more stable lifestyle, and accepting one's responsibilities will relate to the patient's wishes, ROs, and RSs. Anxieties and resistances to change will become very evident around this issue.

Relapse.   During the middle phase of treatment, careful attention should be paid to any relapse. Drug and alcohol addiction is a chronic, relapsing disorder. Modern theory concerning relapse is that relapses are part of recovery. The fact of the relapse permits examination of the patient's response to it. That is, one can respond well or poorly to a relapse. A poor response is to take the attitude, "Well, I relapsed last night. Now I might as well continue to use, drop out of treatment, etc." A more positive response would be: "I relapsed last night. Now I must discuss what happened with my therapist [counselor, sponsor]. What was I feeling toward others and myself that preceded using?" The CCRT can be used to provide greater understanding of the meaning of the patient's use and permit expression of the patient's shame, guilt, and tendency to devalue others.

Participation in self-help groups.   The therapist should never become dogmatic about AA, NA, or CA attendance. Some patients never become engaged in a 12-step group but do well with psychotherapy. Others take time to get used to and experience the benefits of 12-step programs. As with other aspects of treatment, the therapist's flexibility around 12-step involvement leaves him or her free to acknowledge that people are different and what works for one does not necessarily work for others. Nevertheless, for the patient who has chronic problems refraining from drug use, 12-step involvement should be strongly encouraged. Patients should be reminded that the 12-step program can be available to them long after therapy has ended. Often the CCRT can also be used to examine a particular patient's reluctance to engage in a self-help group. ROs that involve anticipations that people in a group will not like or accept the patient can be expected to impede the patient's willingness to give the group a try.

Last Phase

It is important to remember that the conclusion of time-limited treatment does not mean the end of the process of recovery. In general, the patient should also be involved in some ongoing therapeutic relationship. Thus, one goal of treatment is for the patient to become invested in a social network that can sustain him or her, help avoid isolation, and provide practical help in minimizing or avoiding a relapse. As with any other dynamic therapy, the therapist can expect to deal with the patient's ambivalence toward ending therapy. Substance abusers may have more difficulty dealing with ambivalence than many other patients. Addicted patients may experience ambivalence, anxiety, and other uncomfortable states as a reason to use in an effort to minimize the discomfort. The therapist should not be overly anxious about termination and should help the patient to anticipate and express possible negative feelings associated with continuing the recovery process on his or her own.

Transference and Countertransference

As with any dynamic therapy approach, the role of transference holds a central position in the approach to substance abuse treatment presented here. Also as described in other chapters, the terms *transference* and *countertransference* refer to what is said and done in sessions by the patient and therapist that has implications and reverberations for the therapeutic relationship and that relates to the patient's central relationship issues. The patient's reactions to the therapist figure prominently in the patient's ROs and RSs as identified in the patient's CCRT.

For example, the patient's reaction to a relatively straightforward action on the part of the therapist, such as recommending attendance at AA or NA, may vary from experiencing the therapist as caring to seeing him or her as rejecting or controlling. If the therapist congratulates the patient on his or her first month of sobriety, the therapist could be perceived as an ally, as condescending, or as irrelevant. Outside of therapy, these types of patient reactions are typically left unsaid and are usually so automatic and seem so self-evident to the patient that he or she does not recognize that these are judgments placed on reality, rather than reality itself.

In the face of these sometimes intense reactions by the patient, the therapist can find him- or herself having reciprocal reactions. If the patient is intimidating, it is natural to feel intimidated. If the patient is acting as though he or she is superior to the therapist, it is natural for the therapist to feel resentful. These countertransference reactions can be used to infer the reactions of others who experience the patient's interpersonal style.[1]

It is important to understand that it is not useful to explore each and every transference manifestation. The focus of the therapy session should be the patient, his or her current life situation, and how the patient's substance abuse affects his or her life. Neverthe-

---

[1] The therapist's attitudes described earlier, of disgust or pity toward patients with substance abuse problems, also represent a type of countertransference. In this section, we are most interested in the therapist's specific reactions that are essentially "elicited" from a particular patient's interpersonal style.

less, it is sometimes quite necessary for the therapist to draw out and make explicit the nature of the patient's transference. According to this model of treatment, transference-countertransference relationship issues should be taken up when such an examination may illuminate concerns outside therapy or when something about the patient-therapist interaction is preventing a meaningful exchange from occurring. Relating this reaction back to earlier discussions of the CCRT can be useful for both of these situations. If, for instance, the patient's RO anticipates scorn and ridicule from others, this may underlie her unwillingness to discuss with the therapist a shameful incident when she was intoxicated. This reluctance to trust the therapist may illustrate her difficulty trusting a new, sober boyfriend who wants to get closer to her. Use of transference interpretations can provide a very useful, in vivo experience for the patient but should be used cautiously by novice therapists and should take place under the supervision of an experienced dynamic psychotherapist.

■ CLINICAL ILLUSTRATION

The case described here is that of time-limited (6 months) supportive-expressive treatment for cocaine abuse during which the patient was seen twice weekly (9, 10). Mr. H was an unmarried, 26-year-old, lower-level manager at a midsized factory. He owned his own home and permitted a male friend to live there rent free. Mr. H had used a variety of substances recreationally for 10 years, but his cocaine use had increased dramatically in the 2 years before treatment. He reported having felt depressed since high school. Mr. H also reported never having had a girlfriend and never having had sex without paying for it. He insisted that his cocaine use was not a problem and that he would leave treatment if the therapist made it an issue. This latter statement is regularly encountered in such treatments, even though, as with Mr. H, there was ample evidence that his cocaine use resulted in missing work and decreased work motivation. His absences and poor work performance eventually led to suspension from his job and then loss of his house. After a particularly severe binge 2 months into therapy, he was able to acknowledge an overwhelming desire to use cocaine.

Transference Implications

The case summary reveals how quickly the transference can become manifest in the therapeutic relationship. Mr. H implied that his staying in treatment was somehow the therapist's responsibility by his initial insistence that cocaine was not a problem and that any effort on the therapist's part to address this issue would result in his fleeing therapy. Immediately in the first session, the therapist felt controlled and threatened. The therapist chose not to respond from this countertransference, which might have resulted in an argument with the patient. Rather, exploration of the patient's interactions with others revealed a pattern in which the patient tended to get what he wanted from others (understanding, pity) by insisting on setting the conditions of the interactions, "or else." His tendency to respond by exploding and fleeing whenever he encountered difficult or uncomfortable situations typically resulted in making matters worse rather than better. By patiently exploring such reactions, the therapist was able to get the patient to acknowledge these patterns and the negative effect they had on his life.

Mr. H's Core Conflictual Relationship Theme

Mr. H's central wish was an intense desire for closeness, love, and affection but he had no idea of how to build such relationships. His central RS, in addition to using cocaine and being depressed, was a self-image of being a fool, interpersonally incompetent, and unlikable. His central affective states were shame and humiliation. In light of this negative self-evaluation, his only recourse to achieve his wish (love, affection) was to "buy" friendship with drugs, money, or gifts (i.e., buying drugs for groups of "friends" or having his male friend live in his home rent free). Not surprisingly, he often ended up feeling exploited and would feel humiliated, explode, and flee the relationship. One method of fleeing the scene was to get high. The central negative RO was that he would be exploited. Consider how the CCRT and transference are played out in the following vignette.[2]

Mr. H, who pays at the end of each session, wrote out a check larger than the agreed-on fee. The therapist put the check aside without observing the amount until later. The next session began:

> *Therapist:* I noticed you wrote out a check for [amount of check] last time we met.
>
> *Patient:* I thought you deserved it. It was an important session to me.
>
> *Therapist:* Yes, and I'm glad that it was. But still, is it a question that you would pay me extra for it?
>
> *Patient:* I don't know; I wanted you to have it.
>
> *Therapist:* You know, doesn't this seem like when you buy Lisa and Ruth dinner or Stephanie flowers? As with them, you want to let me know you appreciated something, that something happened in here that was important to you, but it gets expressed in the medium of money, with a gift.
>
> *Patient:* And then I feel taken advantage of.

In this vignette, the wish to get close to someone, to have some affection and appreciation pass between him and another person, is expressed obliquely. Rather than having his wish satisfied, he typically ends up feeling exploited, a pattern transferred from one situation to another.

Noted in Mr. H's CCRT was his tendency to use threats to

---

[2]Excerpted from Mark D, Luborsky L: *A Manual for the Use of Supportive-Expressive Psychotherapy in the Treatment of Cocaine Abuse.* Unpublished manual, Department of Psychiatry, Hospital of the University of Pennsylvania, 1992. Used with permission.

control people and, when faced with difficult, uncomfortable situations, to flee from, avoid, or deny the difficulty. Indeed, after an explosive altercation with friends, he disappeared for a week, flying to another city without telling anyone. In the course of therapy he had threatened suicide during anxiety-provoking moments. During one session, after he had lost his job, the therapist asked when Mr. H intended to attempt a return to work—he had been drug free for 3 months but had made no attempt to return to work. Mr. H began the next session by saying that it was time to terminate therapy. The therapist was aware of Mr. H's lifelong tendency to threaten extreme behavior when things did not go how he wanted them to or when others disappointed him. The therapist's understanding of the anxiety and distress brought about by the therapist's introduction of the topic of work permitted him to empathically stay with the patient. When Mr. H "threatened" to terminate the therapy, the therapist responded:

Therapist: Can you recall what we talked about last time?
Patient: No.

This did not surprise the therapist. It simply reflected Mr. H's tendency to avoid troubling topics. As the therapist reminded the patient of the discussion about work, the dialogue continued:

Patient: This talk about work is going nowhere. I don't
    really care about work. Let's just leave it at that.
Therapist: You want to drop the topic?
Patient: I would be more depressed if I worked.
Therapist: Could you say more about that?

By saying that he feared depression if he worked, Mr. H gave the therapist the opportunity to explore the meaning of his need to threaten to leave therapy. Later, when Mr. H said he "dreaded" work, the therapist asked:

> *Therapist:* Should we try and understand what this fear is
> about? Is there another way, other than dropping the
> matter altogether?
>
> *Patient:* I've never done that before.
>
> *Therapist:* Well, let's see if we can get hold of it. Tell me
> more about your dread about this situation, of returning
> to work.

At this point, the patient and the therapist begin a meaningful discussion of his relationships at work. In particular, he was afraid of returning to work where he had been discharged because of poor performance while using cocaine at work. At termination, Mr. H had been drug free for about 4 months and had begun to work. He had connected with a sponsor and was regularly attending NA meetings. He reported being less explosive with others. Mr. H had not yet been able to form a meaningful relationship with a woman. He was able to acknowledge, however, that his chances for improvement in this area were better while he stayed sober.

■ EMPIRICAL FINDINGS

As stated previously, there is empirical support suggesting that people with substance and psychological problems benefit from psychotherapy. In addition, there is good evidence that Luborsky's supportive-expressive therapy is effective in the treatment of opiate addiction (8). An NIDA-funded, multisite, controlled clinical trial, the NIDA Collaborative Cocaine Treatment Study, is currently investigating the effectiveness of the supportive-expressive treatment for cocaine described above (15).

■ RELEVANCE FOR MANAGED CARE

Supportive-expressive therapy with substance-abusing patients has been tested in clinical trials on opiate-addicted patients and is currently being tested for cocaine-addicted patients. These treatments, although time limited, utilize more sessions than are often covered under some managed care plans. The NIDA Collaborative Cocaine Treatment Study (15), for instance, utilizes 6 months of treatment, with sessions held twice a week for the first 3 months, for a total of about 36 sessions. However, the clinical trials testing supportive-expressive treatment for opiate dependence provided 6 months of weekly treatment, or about 24 sessions (8). These are both higher than the availability of 20 sessions per annum that is typically available through health maintenance organizations.

Therapists should also be aware that some managed care companies "carve out" substance abuse from mental health coverage. In some instances, substance abuse is covered only for medical detoxification, so only patients with a mental health diagnosis, such as anxiety or depression, will be covered for treatment. Such arbitrary and (from a treatment perspective) irrational demarcations between mental health and substance abuse problems can clearly have an impact on the amount of treatment available to an individual patient.

It is our opinion that, despite these frustrating restrictions, therapists should not be dissuaded by limitations on coverage for therapy. Quite a lot can be done in 20 sessions, and some things can be accomplished in fewer sessions. With severe restrictions on sessions, it may be wise to use more sessions early, when sobriety is less stable and the therapeutic alliance needs to be established. Spreading sessions out during the later middle and last stages of treatment, especially if things are going better, gives the patient time to experience his or her sobriety and to bring in problems to discuss with the therapist. Session restrictions also mean that the therapist must be sure to work with the patient around availing himself or herself of self-help and other community programs.

■ REFERENCES

1. Barber JP, Crits-Christoph P: Comparison of the brief dynamic therapies, in Handbook of Short-Term Dynamic Psychotherapy. Edited by Crits-Christoph P, Barber JP. New York, Basic Books, 1991, pp 323–352

2. Strupp HH, Binder JL: Psychotherapy in a New Key. New York, Basic Books, 1984

3. Budman SH, Gurman AS: Theory and Practice of Brief Therapy. New York, Guilford, 1988

4. Valliant GE: Dangers of psychotherapy in the treatment of alcoholism, in Dynamic Approaches to the Understanding and Treatment of Alcoholism. Edited by Bean MH, Zinberg NE. New York, Free Press, 1981, pp 36–54

5. Dodes LM: Abstinence from alcohol in long-term individual psychotherapy with alcoholics. Am J Psychother 38:248–256, 1984

6. Luborsky L, McLellan AT, Woody GE, et al: Therapist success and its determinants. Arch Gen Psychiatry 42:602–611, 1985

7. Levin JD: Psychodynamic treatment of alcohol abuse, in Dynamic Therapies for Psychiatric Disorders: Axis I. Edited by Barber JP, Crits-Christoph P. New York, Basic Books, 1995, pp 193–229

8. Luborsky L, Woody GE, Hole AV, et al: Supportive-expressive dynamic therapy for treatment of opiate drug dependence, in Dynamic Therapies for Psychiatric Disorders: Axis I. Edited by Barber JP, Crits-Christoph P. New York, Basic Books, 1995, pp 131–160

9. Mark D, Faude J: Supportive-expressive therapy of cocaine abuse, in Dynamic Therapies for Psychiatric Disorders: Axis I. Edited by Barber JP, Crits-Christoph P. New York, Basic Books, 1995, pp 294–331

10. Mark D, Luborsky L: A Manual for the Use of Supportive-Expressive Psychotherapy in the Treatment of Cocaine Abuse. Unpublished manual, Department of Psychiatry, Hospital of the University of Pennsylvania, 1992

11. Zweben J: Recovery-oriented psychotherapy: a model for addiction treatment. Psychotherapy 30:259–268, 1993

12. Woody GE, McLellan AT, Luborsky L, et al: Sociopathy and psychotherapy outcome. Arch Gen Psychiatry 40:1081–1086, 1985

13. Trimpey J: Rational Recovery: The New Cure for Substance Addiction. New York, Pocket Books, 1996

14. Luborsky L: Principles of Psychoanalytic Psychotherapy: A Manual for Supportive Expressive Treatment. New York, Basic Books, 1984

15. Crits-Christoph P, Siqueland L, Blaine J, et al: The NIDA Cocaine Collaborative Treatment Study: rationale and methods. Arch Gen Psychiatry (in press)

CONSIDER THIS APPROACH FOR CHILDREN WHO:

- Are of preschool or early school age with elimination disorders
- Have situational depression and anxiety
- Have behavior problems related to a developmental crisis, such as the birth of a sibling
- Have somatic symptoms associated with transition into school or day care
- Have uncomplicated separation anxiety disorder
- Have an adjustment disorder associated with an environmental loss, such as divorce

8

BRIEF PSYCHODYNAMIC PSYCHOTHERAPY WITH CHILDREN

Child psychiatry has enjoyed a long tradition of using brief psychodynamic psychotherapy with children. In 1909, one of Freud's seminal case descriptions, "Little Hans," concerned a latency-age boy treated indirectly for a phobia over a period of just 4 months (1). As is true throughout the history of psychiatry, however, advances in treatments for children have lagged behind comparable developments in adult psychiatry. Thus, the child guidance movement, which made psychotherapy accessible to children in their communities, began to flourish only some two decades after the mental hygiene movement started in the United States in the early 1900s. By the middle of this century, however, children were routinely being seen in individual psychodynamic psychotherapy, some for prolonged treatment and often independent of any intervention for the parents or family. At the same time, many children were being seen in treatments of 20 sessions or fewer that also included work with the parents. The proponents of this briefer approach were convinced that it was both efficacious and of lasting benefit (2, 3).

Whereas the underpinnings of modern American psychiatry are strongly influenced by object relations theory (4), European child psychiatry remained closer to its psychoanalytic roots. Even in Europe, however, children were being seen in brief treatments

This chapter was written specifically for this book by Robert Racusin, M.D., Associate Professor of Psychiatry at Dartmouth Medical School, Princeton, New Jersey.

based firmly in psychoanalytic principles. The most important contributor to this work was D. W. Winnicott, who often needed only one to three sessions to engage in a therapeutic dialogue with children from an "average expectable environment" (5). Using his still-current "Squiggle Game" technique along with parent guidance, Winnicott believed that a brief therapeutic encounter would enable many children to return to a normal developmental trajectory once maladaptive beliefs and patterns of behavior could be identified and corrected.

Until recently, developments in brief psychotherapy for children grew largely out of clinical experience and were neither applied nor studied systematically. As a result, when the demand for accountability and demonstration of efficacy began to affect the level of psychiatric benefits available in many managed and capitated health plans, psychodynamic psychotherapy for children was often either overlooked or equated with long-term, analytically oriented treatment for adults. In fact, studies have long shown that treatment of children for as few as 12 sessions has been beneficial and cost-effective for selected children (6, 7).

At present, there appears to be a trend toward developing highly structured, manualized, behavioral treatments for homogeneous groups of child patients (8) as a way of keeping therapy brief. As is described in this chapter, however, there is also a place for circumscribed but dynamically informed treatment that is tailored to an individual's intrapsychic and family structure rather than to a categorical diagnosis.

■ CONCEPTUAL MATTERS ESSENTIAL TO BRIEF PSYCHODYNAMIC PSYCHOTHERAPY WITH CHILDREN

The Developmental Perspective

One of the defining characteristics of childhood is that it is a time of change and growth. Physical, cognitive, emotional, linguistic, interpersonal, and intrapsychic development are complexly interrelated, and periods of rapid change are intermixed with periods of relative stability. Furthermore, the pace, direction, and evenness of development are influenced by both endogenous (e.g., genetic endowment, congenital characteristics) and exogenous (e.g., nutrition, experience) factors. As a result, no two children, even monozygotic twins, follow the exact same developmental course.

At the same time, however, overall patterns tend to be quite similar within large populations of children. When children are assessed for behavioral or emotional problems, therefore, it is essential to determine whether the problems, for example, as defined by parents, represent normal development (or a normal developmental variation) or a maladaptive response. Behaviors and conflicts that are developmentally normal are best treated with parent guidance rather than psychotherapy for the child.

Play is one of the universal developmental landmarks of childhood and serves a variety of important functions for children. In addition to being a self-reinforcing source of pleasure, it is important as a way for children to safely discharge drive energy, even though they are physically vulnerable; to gain a sense of mastery over a complicated and sometimes frightening environment; to practice the adult roles that they must someday assume; to experiment safely with different solutions to interpersonal conflict; to safely express feelings, fears, and conflicts for which they as yet do not have the verbal skills to express; and to experience the pleasures and challenges of being part of a peer group.

The key to being able to use play in the service of healthy development is the capacity to use fantasy (9). Children not only use fantasy and displacement to express unacceptable feelings and wishes but also respond to others who are sharing the play. This is the basis for much interpersonal fantasy play, in which two or more children work out action and dialogue as seriously as any playwrights but without ever having to step out into "the real world" to talk about the fact that they are creating a fantasy. Much psychotherapeutic work with children takes advantage of the child's ability to utilize fantasy and displacement to deal with affect and content that is "off limits" to the child in the "real world."

The Systems Perspective

D. W. Winnicott once wrote that "[t]he infant and the maternal care together form a unit" (10). The implication of Winnicott's observation is true of people of all ages. No one can be fully understood outside the family and social context of which he or she is a part. Family systems are characterized by reciprocity and complementarity of adaptive behaviors. In other words, families work together to maintain equilibrium at both the systems and intrapsychic levels.

It is not surprising, therefore, that children's symptoms often serve the dual function of expressing both individual and systems dynamics. An understanding of this multilevel determinism is essential for devising interventions that involve parents as well as children. For some families, parent education is sufficient to alter parental behavior that contributes to children's maladaptive responses. Other families require more intensive interventions, including parent guidance, individual parent therapy, couples counseling, or family treatment. For families falling at the healthier end of the spectrum, brief psychodynamic psychotherapy with children can often include parents as mediators of treatment in a way that corrects the intrafamilial patterns that are exacerbating the child's difficulty.

■ COMPREHENSIVE ASSESSMENT

The Biopsychosocial Approach

A prerequisite for any treatment of a child with brief psychodynamic psychotherapy is a comprehensive assessment of the child's physiological status and intrapsychic and family functioning. This is necessary to accomplish the following goals:

- Appreciate the relative contribution of the multiple determinants of the child's symptoms
- Develop a correspondingly appropriate formulation of the treatment focus
- Identify areas of strength and competence that can be enlisted in helping the child develop new coping skills
- Identify other areas of developmental interference that require concomitant or subsequent evaluation and intervention

The simultaneous consideration of these various factors has been referred to as the *biopsychosocial approach* (11).

Gathering the necessary clinical data as dictated by the biopsychosocial approach requires a systematic assessment procedure. Although the sequence and techniques of data gathering may vary among patients and among clinicians, a typical evaluation includes several aspects (Table 8–1).

Multimodal and Multidisciplinary Treatment Planning

The development of a treatment strategy for short-term dynamic psychotherapy is described in detail later in this chapter. For many children, the most cost-effective plan will be multimodal and multidisciplinary. Therefore, it is essential that additional treatment approaches be carefully and fully considered. Questions to be asked in this regard include, for example, the following:

- Should the child be considered for psychotropic medication?
- Should the parents be seen for couples counseling?
- Does the child need classroom accommodations or special education services?
- Does the family need help from a social service agency?

When treatment is complex and involves several professionals, the identification of a case manager who is responsible for coordinating services, locating funding for services, and maintaining

---

TABLE 8–1. **Systematic assessment**

Standardized behavioral and history questionnaires completed by parents before and/or at the time of the initial appointment, for example:

- A demographic, developmental, and/or health inventory
- Parent/teacher assessments of the child's behavior (e.g., the Child Behavior Checklist[a])
- Inventories for specific disorders (e.g., the Post-Traumatic Stress Disorder Checklist—Parent Form[b] for posttraumatic stress disorder)

Initial family interview to obtain

- Background information about the presenting problem
- Attempts already made to ameliorate the symptoms
- Organization of family and how members communicate

Individual interview with the identified child patient to

- Establish rapport
- Assess the child's perception of the problem
- Evaluate the child's developmental strengths and weaknesses
- Understand the child's temperament and defensive/coping style
- Estimate the child's ability to use fantasy in the service of psychodynamic treatment
- Test the child's readiness and motivation for behavioral change

A parent interview (usually both parents/guardians together) to

- Obtain further developmental history
- Evaluate parent/child dynamics in symptom formation and maintenance
- Assess the capacity of the parents to participate as mediators of family change

Collateral information from school, day care providers, physicians, and others who have relevant data about the child, both longitudinally and in different settings

(continued)

TABLE 8–1.   **Systematic assessment** *(continued)*

Additional evaluation procedures when indicated by the history or
clinical assessment (e.g., neuroimaging for possible seizures)

A family feedback meeting to

- Review the results of the assessment
- Explain the procedure and focus of short-term psychodynamic
  treatment
- Make other treatment recommendations as needed

[a] Achenbach TM: *Empirically Based Taxonomy.* Burlington, University of Vermont Department of Psychiatry, 1992.
[b] Dartmouth Child Trauma Research Group: *PTSD Checklist for Children— Parent Report.* White River Junction, VT, National Center for Post-Traumatic Stress Disorder, 1997.

good communication among all the providers and the family may
be key to the treatment plan's successful implementation.

■ PATIENT SELECTION

Brief psychodynamic psychotherapy with children works best with
children who have a circumscribed set of symptoms or specific
developmental interference that is related to a "central (internalized) conflict" that, in turn, has been identified during the comprehensive assessment described above. Whether the conflict is
formulated in terms of structural conflict (e.g., id versus superego
with ego-mediated symptom formation), family systems theory
(e.g., triangulation of parental conflict), or an object relations
paradigm (e.g., Winnicott's "false-self" adaptation [12]), it is seen
as being expressed in a limited number of behaviors (e.g., angry
outbursts when frustrated, soiling, stomach aches on school mornings, difficulty falling asleep, or sadness or irritability after visits
with a noncustodial parent). Although this approach is suitable for
a wide range of children, there are a few exclusion criteria (Table
8–2).

TABLE 8–2.	**Exclusion criteria**

Brief psychodynamic psychotherapy is not suited for children who

- Have a pervasive developmental disorder
- Have comorbid untreated attention-deficit/hyperactivity disorder
- Are dangerously aggressive or self-destructive
- Lack a capacity for symbolic, communicative play
- Lack a sense of basic trust in or attachment to their human environment (e.g., children who have been abused or neglected), unless the treatment is adjunctive to a long-term intervention with a consistently present therapist
- Lack environmental stability and safety (e.g., live in homes characterized by domestic violence, parental substance abuse, or frequent losses of caregiving adults)

On the other hand, this approach is useful even with children who have multiple developmental impairments, comorbid psychopathology, and coexisting physical illness when they also have

- A stable, supportive family
- The prospect of active parental involvement in the treatment
- A strong motivation for symptom relief
- Generally adequate coping abilities despite multiple symptoms or developmental problems

■ TECHNIQUE

Determining the Treatment Focus and Engaging the Child and Family

Treatment goals should be both general and specific. For most children, general goals include some combination of symptom reduction, the promotion of normal development, the fostering of autonomy and self-reliance, and environmental change, such as at school or home. A specific goal for the child is to "become ready" to accomplish some developmental task or adaptive behavior that he or she ambivalently wishes to do (and is physically and cognitively capable of performing) but is presently being prevented from doing by feelings of sadness or fear, a lack of skill or practice, or worry or anxiety about performance. This goal is the therapist's statement to the child of both the nature of the central conflict and its relationship to the symptom(s). For the parents, specific goals are defined in terms of particular roles or tasks, such as devising a way to recognize the patient's status as "older brother" by assigning a slightly later bedtime or the privilege of assisting the parent with a more "grown-up" task than is permitted for younger siblings.

Engaging the child and family to accomplish these goals is essential for the formation of a treatment alliance, which in turn empowers the therapist to help the child and the family. Therefore, it is of paramount importance that the alliance be nurtured from the first contact with the patient and family. The first step in the formation of this alliance is the therapist's willingness to listen to everything the patient and family have to say about the presenting problem during the initial appointment. This willingness to listen does not mean an unquestioning acceptance of everything that is said. Thorough exploration of the underlying meaning of behavior and feelings is essential. This must be done without judgmental responses from the therapist and with tactful confrontations of the distortions and inconsistencies that inevitably emerge.

The alliance is strengthened by the comprehensiveness of the subsequent assessment, which, because of the breadth and depth of the data, gives the therapist maximal credibility when presenting the biopsychosocial formulation and its derivative, multimodal treatment recommendations. The child and family who have developed a fundamental attitude of trust and confidence in the therapist's competence and wish to be helpful are in the best position to accept the therapist's dynamic formulation and treatment recommendations. For children, this means being willing and able to accept the specific treatment goal described above in terms of "getting ready" to relinquish the symptom once the underlying, psychological obstacles to growth are removed. For parents, acceptance of the formulation and plan means making the commitment to bring the child to the recommended number of sessions (usually 4–20) at the recommended frequency (usually weekly), to support them financially, to attend the recommended number of parent guidance sessions (usually monthly), to implement the changes at home suggested by the therapist, and to candidly report progress (or lack of it) during the meetings with the therapist.

Use of Play Materials

For children, the use of play materials is often an essential factor in establishing rapport and undertaking a "therapeutic dialogue." The use of play materials to facilitate communication should not, however, be confused with "just playing" with the child in the guise of doing psychotherapy. The "tools" of the child psychotherapist include an array of toys that facilitate communication about a variety of topics in a number of different ways.

Toys can generally be divided into two types: semistructured and unstructured. Semistructured toys are those that have a meaning or purpose implied by their structure and function. A well-equipped office will have a number of different types of these, including puppets, dolls and a dollhouse, animals, blocks (wood or Lego-type), and vehicles. It is often helpful to have a combination of "regular" vehicles (trucks, cars), emergency vehicles (fire, police, ambulance), and "long-distance" vehicles (boat, plane, train) because the themes that emerge in this type of treatment often involve topics such as movement, aggression, injury, or abandonment, which can be elaborated further with specific types of toys. Unstructured toys are those with structure or function that do not suggest a particular meaning or purpose. An adequate selection of these might include a sand tray, colored pens and paper, and clay. Drawing materials are most frequently used and are the most flexible and the least messy.

Use of Verbal and Nonverbal Interventions

The technique of brief psychodynamic psychotherapy relies on a combination of verbal, nonverbal, and mixed verbal and nonverbal interventions. In general, the degree to which these interventions make use of fantasy and displacement is inversely proportional to the age of the child. Even for the oldest preadolescents, however, it is usual to make considerable use of these processes. An example of a verbal intervention in displacement is an interpretation within the fantasy, for example, the statement that "that little girl [doll] is really disappointed that she has to go to bed by herself." Examples of nonverbal interventions include interactions, or play in which the therapist uses a toy figure or a drawing to respond to some action of the child; parallel play, in which the therapist engages in an activity similar to or imitative of the child's play in an effort to establish rapport; and rolling or throwing a soft ball for the same purpose. Mixed verbal and nonverbal interventions include reciprocal drawing activities followed by an explanatory narrative, as is exemplified beautifully in Winnicott's "Squiggle Game."

The purpose of these interventions usually falls into one of the following four categories:

1. Classification/reflection of affect
2. Classification/reflection of preconscious or unconscious psychic material
3. Establishing a conscious connection between symptoms and other mental phenomena
4. Helping the child devise alternative adaptive strategies in lieu of symptoms

Before children can change behavior, they often need to develop an awareness of and vocabulary for important feelings that are not being expressed directly. Thus, many of the initial interventions in dynamic psychotherapy are designed to give words and names to feelings as well as to assign attribution.

Children who are able to describe and attribute affect may not have conscious awareness of the memories, thoughts, and/or wishes that accompany the feelings that they are expressing in their play. As part of their attempts at adaptation that have precipitated the core conflict and its symptoms, certain of these memories, thoughts, and wishes have been repressed because they have been deemed unacceptably threatening to the self. Typical of such mental content are regressive, aggressive, and oedipal wishes. Once affect and the associated memories, wishes, and thoughts have been articulated, the child is still often unaware of the connection between these associations and specific symptoms and behaviors. This is the result of how successful symptoms can usually be in blocking awareness of unacceptable mental content. Again, in displacement, the therapist is frequently called on to intervene in a way that makes these connections conscious, for example, pointing out that "when the doll is angry at her parents for being too busy, she feels like hitting her little brother, even though she's really mad at her mommy and daddy." Once these connections are made conscious in the play, children often spontaneously move from displacement to personal reality and say something such as "That's just like me." Not all children reach this point, however, and it is not always necessary that they do. Clinical experience has shown that some children are able to "work through" conflict and symptom resolution entirely by way of the therapeutic dialogue in displacement.

Finally, children often need to use the play situation to develop alternative, adaptive strategies to replace the symptoms that are being relinquished. This makes sense because the symptom was formed initially because of a lack of a more adaptive solution to an interpersonal problem. Thus, in the example of the angry older sister in the preceding paragraph, the therapist is likely to wonder aloud "What else could the doll do to show her parents how she felt?" This will usually be followed by a discussion of various alternatives and their potential outcomes from the perspective of how the patient would anticipate them in her own family. At this point, too, many children identify the "reality" of the play as it relates to their own lives, whereas others will not do so consciously in the therapy.

Transference and the "Corrective Emotional Experience"

The elucidation of transference is usually not the goal in brief dynamic psychotherapy with children unless the feelings and attributions brought by the child into the therapy are of such negative intensity as to interfere with the formation of the treatment alliance. Thus, for example, the child who, on the basis of previous experiences with adult caretakers, expects his expressions of fearfulness to be met with criticism or ridicule may become entrenched in a resentful, self-protective silence whenever the therapist introduces the question of fearfulness in response to the child's play. Alternatively, the child may even refuse to participate in play activities altogether as a defensive maneuver to avoid expected adult criticism. These obstacles of fear, anger, and guilt need to be recognized, understood, made conscious, and dealt with before the treatment can proceed. One of the important benefits of doing a comprehensive evaluation as described above is that the existence of negative transference obstacles will almost inevitably appear during the assessment phase. For some children, these negative reactions to adults are so deeply rooted that the child cannot be considered a good candidate for this type of treatment and needs to be referred for an alternative type of intervention.

Most children for whom brief treatment is appropriate bring with them a generally positive set of expectations and feelings in their relationships with adults, even if they have experienced considerable anger, criticism, or frustration with respect to the presenting symptoms. The therapist's stance of acceptance and hopefulness even about the symptoms in question offers the child a "corrective emotional experience," that is, an opportunity to avoid shame in the presence of an adult who "knows everything" about the child's problems. This alternative to what the child has become used to feeling and thinking facilitates, in turn, a powerful motivation on the part of the child for further uncovering and exploration in the therapy. This approach also supports the child's ability to take the psychological risk of giving up familiar behavioral patterns (the symptoms) in favor of newer, more adaptive behaviors, which, because of their unfamiliarity, almost always are undertaken with apprehension, if not frank anxiety.

■ CLINICAL ILLUSTRATIONS

J. was a girl of 2 years and 11 months who was living with her parents and only sibling, a younger brother of 1 year and 2 months. J. had been referred by her pediatrician for evaluation and treatment of stool withholding of 3.5 months' duration, despite a vigorous regimen of stool softeners, reassurance, and behavioral reinforcement for using the toilet.

History revealed no problems with elimination or other behaviors before the abrupt onset of her stool-withholding behavior. The appearance of the symptom occurred during a visit with a maternal aunt. J. had already enjoyed several months of full toilet training success before this visit and had visited this same aunt without any toileting difficulties on several occasions in the past. Since the onset of the stool-withholding symptom, however, J. had voluntarily and forcefully withheld her bowel movements despite the use of stool softeners, suppositories, mineral oil, and diet manipulation. She retained bladder control and was able to use either a potty chair or a regular toilet for urinating. She was not enuretic. When she had to have a bowel movement, she insisted on being put into a diaper. She was only rarely encopretic and consistently expressed relief and pleasure after having a bowel movement in her diaper.

Additional history revealed that there was no history of trauma and no history of anxiety associated with elimination in general or with J.'s initial toilet training in particular. Since the onset of her stool withholding, J. had become increasingly interested in seeing other children's bowel movements, especially those of her younger brother. She seemed both fascinated and repelled by feces but did not articulate any specific fears about toilets or bowel movements.

Other aspects of J.'s social development were presented as unremarkable. She was described by her parents as smart, stubborn, self-reliant, happy, and outgoing. She did have some problems with power struggles and temper tantrums during the year before the referral, which were primarily focused around the arrival of her younger brother. These behavioral problems were seen by her parents as developmentally normal, however, and had largely disappeared well before the onset of her stool withholding.

J.'s parents both had full-time jobs outside the home. There was no history of significant family stress or conflict, abuse, interpersonal losses, or significant separation problems. After her initial jealousy of her new brother had subsided, J. had tended to either ignore him or be protective of him. There was no history of any direct expression of anger toward him for many months.

J.'s appetite was good. She had some difficulty falling asleep and had occasional midcycle awakening with nightmares; however, she was easily comforted and able to return to her own bed with parental help. There was no history of phobias, aggression, anhedonia, or bizarre behavior.

A mental status examination showed J. to be a well-developed, neatly dressed, appealing girl with blond hair. She was right-handed and well-coordinated, active, and assertive but directable with gentle verbal limits. She had good receptive language and a good vocabulary for her age. She spoke mainly in phrases but was capable of using sentences. Her speech was somewhat difficult to understand at times because of immature articulation, but she expressed herself well. Her mood was initially apprehensive but soon became positive, and her affect was of full range and was appropriate to the situation. Her thought processes were logical, coherent, and goal directed. There was no evidence of cognitive or neurological impairment.

The diagnostic impression was that J. had an adjustment disorder with a physical symptom secondary to her reaction to the arrival of a new sibling. The central conflict was defined as J.'s inability to express any angry feelings toward her brother in the face of her parents' selective reinforcement of only the positive side of J.'s ambivalence. As a result, J. either acceded to her parents' wishes at the cost of being able to experience both positive and negative affect toward her brother, or she felt "nothing" toward him and ignored him. Her stool withholding was seen as an indirect expression of her anger and as a regressive wish in response to her jealousy.

The treatment plan consisted of four parts:

1. A behavioral management plan taught to J.'s parents for her stool withholding
2. Pediatrician-monitored use of mineral oil and stool softeners as needed to control constipation
3. A family-based intervention whereby her parents would take steps to establish J.'s role as "big sister" at home
4. A series of four individual psychodynamic psychotherapy sessions for J. that would focus on facilitating her recognition and expression of her ambivalence about both her younger brother and her bowel movements, as well as on making conscious for her the relationship between her affect and her wishes and fears about her brother and her behavior

At the beginning of the first of the four scheduled treatment sessions, the therapist met J. in the waiting room with her mother. When her mother was given permission to join the initial part of the session, J. took the therapist's hand and happily walked to the office with her mother several steps behind.

J. quickly became interested in some colored markers, which she used one at a time while identifying the color. After using each one, she carefully replaced its cap before using the next one. She used the colors to make mostly scribbles and circular patterns.

When she had experimented with all the colors, she easily accepted an invitation to explore the dollhouse. She placed a series of dolls on beds to "sleep and wake up," calling an obviously female doll "him" on several occasions. She was particularly interested in the kitchen and the baby character of the doll figures.

While J. was thus engaged, her mother was asked to leave. J. protested minimally but accepted her mother's gentle but firm directive that J. was to remain with the therapist while mother waited in the waiting room nearby. J.'s play was only briefly disrupted by her mother's departure, and she quickly returned to the dollhouse to create a family scenario. In this scenario, a mother doll was comforting a crying baby doll named Terry while J. played with a larger doll named Lissa. J. was very nurturing to Lissa, soothing her with a bottle. She spontaneously had Lissa urinate in the toilet, but denied that Lissa would ever need to have a bowel movement.

J. then moved to the chalkboard, where she became interested in "making a mess and wiping it" by erasing a series of circular, thick chalk scribbles. J. demonstrated this many times for Lissa with much pleasure and excitement. This activity was utilized to make the following verbal intervention: "Look how much Lissa is enjoying how you make a mess and wipe it up." The purpose of this intervention was to verbalize important affect and assign attribution, but to do so in displacement so as not to disrupt the flow of J.'s play.

J. then moved to examine a basket of small stones that children were allowed to play with. She was interested in the stones but voiced concern that they might spill, so she limited herself to removing them one at a time. The next intervention was designed to label affect, articulate a fear, and propose an adaptive solution: "Are you worried that the rocks will make a mess if they spill? It's OK. We can clean them up."

This intervention served to engage J.'s focus directly on the therapist. She began using the toy telephones to make repeated calls to the therapist that consisted almost exclusively of the dialogue "Hi" and "Bye," accompanied by her pleasure at controlling the approach and separation dynamic of the interaction. During this play, J. would intermittently check to make sure that the "mother" was still comforting Terry and that Lissa had her bottle. As long as the babies were being cared for, J. could enjoy herself with the therapist.

As the first session neared an end, aggression appeared directly for the first time in J.'s play. Using a toy boat that was taking people on a trip, she had a female doll, which J. again identified as "him," "shot" off the boat with a pretend gun several times. Her affect was happy but not excited as she did this. When it came time to leave for the day, J. did not want to separate from Lissa but accepted the therapist's offer to care for Lissa in J.'s absence until the next meeting, in 1 week.

In the second session, J. accompanied the therapist to the office after only a moment's hesitation and without her mother. For this session, a sand tray on wheels was already in the office to give J. an opportunity to use an unstructured medium to express herself.

J. was immediately attracted to the sand tray, which contained, in addition to a layer of sand, a small pot for digging. Using some clay that she had ignored during the previous session, J. made a small number of clay balls to drop in the sand (which she decided would be "grass"), roll around, bury, and recover. This activity seemed to be of considerable interest to J. and she repeated it several times, also using some of the rocks from the basket. When some sand was inadvertently spilled from the tray, J. looked mildly concerned but said nothing.

When she had entered the office, J. had noticed the Lissa doll from the previous week but paid scant attention to her. She did, however, insist that the "mother" doll from the previous week again comfort a crying Terry figure. Eventually Terry "fell asleep," and J. began using him in her sand tray game of burial and recovery. As she repeated the process, she began describing Terry as "all gone" each time he was buried, until, after four or five repetitions, he was "all gone" and not recovered. At that point, J.

seemed to lose interest in the play. This play sequence, which appeared to be highly symbolic of the central conflict affecting J.'s symptomatic behavior, resulted in the following verbal intervention: "Sometimes big sisters wish they could be the only children in their family."

J.'s mixed verbal and nonverbal response was to take a large doll, which she identified as "the brother crying," and to begin to gently apply some lip balm, which she took from her pocket, to the baby's mouth. This started as a caring type of play with the doll but soon became more and more aggressive and involved more and more of the doll's body until she was roughly stabbing at the doll with the lip balm container. Another verbal intervention followed this play sequence: "Sometimes big sisters get angry at their baby brothers. Then they might get scared that they did something wrong."

J.'s mixed verbal and nonverbal response to this verbal intervention, which was designed to label and attribute affect as well as to articulate an unconscious fear, was to resume the pretend telephone calls that had established the initial dialogue the previous week. After satisfying herself with this, she moved back to the sand tray and deliberately spilled some sand, looking at the therapist first defiantly and then with apprehension. Reassurance and problem-solving seemed to be the most important response to provide to J. at that point: "That's OK. We can clean it up if it's a mess." J. visibly relaxed after this was said and, for the remainder of the session, played happily with a variety of toys that she had not previously explored.

Between the second and third sessions, J.'s mother contacted me by telephone to report that J. had spontaneously started using the toilet and had started calling her brother names, mostly "poo-poo head." J.'s mother was encouraged to tolerate this verbal expression of J.'s feelings toward her brother and to follow through on the other aspects of the treatment plan, including the parent visit planned after J.'s final individual psychotherapy session.

For her third session, J. came happily to the office. Because she made no spontaneous reference to the changes reported by her mother, the therapist told J. of her mother's call and asked for J.'s account of what was happening at home. J. acknowledged what her mother had described, with an attitude of "Of course, so what's the big deal?" in response to the therapist's suggestion that she must be pleased with what she had accomplished. J. no longer had any interest in the sand tray or in making messes. Her play was focused entirely on the dollhouse, which she used to create a series of happy, domestic family scenes from everyday life.

The fourth session was taken up with a review of what we had done together. J. remembered each session in detail and was happy to "reminisce" about how she had enjoyed playing with the different toys. She also was happy to report continued success with her use of the toilet and to report that her brother was "years" away from being able to use the toilet himself and, perhaps, would never master its use.

The parents kept their final appointment several weeks later and confirmed J.'s progress. The name-calling of her brother had begun to subside without parental intervention. The parents were satisfied with the outcome and agreed to return if problems developed in the future.

■ EMPIRICAL FINDINGS

Empirical study of the effectiveness and efficacy of psychotherapy with children has generally lagged far behind that of adult treatment (13). As Messer and Warren (14) point out, the pertinent research literature is "remarkably sparse," even though studies indicate that on average children receive six or fewer outpatient sessions (15). There is evidence emerging, however, that brief psychodynamic psychotherapy will prove to be effective for many children and adolescents. These data are converging from several directions.

First, the overall benefit of psychotherapy for children and adolescents has been well established. For example, four meta-analytic reviews between 1985 and 1993 of child and adolescent psychotherapy have shown consistently positive treatment effects across a variety of problems and types of intervention, comparable with meta-analyses of adult psychotherapy (16). Second, there are now data specifically showing the effectiveness of brief psychodynamic treatment with children. Smyrnios and Kirkby (17) compared brief versus time-unlimited psychodynamic treatment of children and their parents, using a brief treatment similar in many respects to that described in this chapter. Both treatment groups showed a significant postintervention decrease in target symptoms and significant improvement on measures of goal attainment. The improvement at the 4-year follow-up assessment was as robust for the brief treatment group as for the children in time-unlimited therapy.

Finally, studies are beginning to focus not only on treatment efficacy (how a treatment works in controlled, laboratory conditions), but on treatment effectiveness (how a treatment works in heterogeneous samples in naturalistic settings) (18). Weisz et al. (16), for example, point out that several well-developed behavioral treatments are now being shown to maintain their effectiveness when they are exported into community treatment environments. It is to be hoped that the future of empirical research in psychodynamic treatment will include similar studies.

■ RELEVANCE FOR MANAGED CARE

Interventions most valued by managed care are "characterized by being affable, affordable, accessible, competent, efficient, and cost-effective" (19, p. 3). Furthermore, "managed care–friendly" treatments are likely to be those that involve patients and families in their own care, which can be used intermittently when symptoms appear or worsen and that result in a high level of patient and family satisfaction. By way of contrast, managed care is unlikely to be hospitable to treatments that are of indeterminate length, tend to exclude parents, and entail procedures that are difficult to describe in the form of a "manual" that can be used by practitioners.

The approach described in this chapter is a modification of "traditional" psychodynamic treatment of children that adheres closely to many of the managed care values noted above. Families are likely to be highly satisfied with an intervention that, in addition to being brief and inclusive of both parents and children, includes a comprehensive initial assessment that focuses on the individual child as well as the family system. As part of a multimodal approach in most cases, brief psychodynamic psychotherapy with children is also compatible with other manual-based psychosocial treatments as well as with pharmacotherapy. To be used effectively within managed care systems, however, it is essential that primary care physicians have clear guidelines for its indications, that therapists recognize that the primary care physician retains overall responsibility for the child's care, and that physicians and therapists communicate closely throughout treatment in order to support the family's attitude of hopefulness and cooperation, which is necessary for treatment to succeed.

■ REFERENCES

1. Freud S: Analysis of a five-year-old boy (1909), in The Sexual Enlightenment of Children. Edited by Rieff P. New York, Collier Books, 1968, pp 47–183
2. Allen FH: Psychotherapy With Children. New York, WW Norton, 1942
3. Moustakas CE: Psychotherapy With Children: The Living Relationship. New York, Harper, 1959
4. Greenberg JR, Mitchell SA: Object Relations in Psychoanalytic Theory. Cambridge, MA, Harvard University Press, 1983
5. Winnicott DW: Therapeutic Consultations in Child Psychiatry. New York, Basic Books, 1971
6. Leventhal T, Weinberger G: Evaluation of a large-scale brief therapy program for children. Am J Orthopsychiatry 45:119–133, 1975
7. Rosenthal AJ, Levine S: Brief psychotherapy with children: process of therapy. Am J Psychiatry 128:141–146, 1971

8. March JS, Mulle K, Herbel B: Behavioral psychotherapy for children and adolescents with obsessive-compulsive disorder. J Am Acad Child Adolesc Psychiatry 33:333–341, 1994

9. Sarnoff C: Latency. New York, Jason Aronson, 1976

10. Winnicott DW: The Maturational Process and the Facilitating Environment. New York, International Universities Press, 1965

11. Engel G: The need for a new medical model: a challenge for biomedicine. Family Systems Medicine 10:317–331, 1992

12. Guntrip H: Psychoanalytic Theory, Therapy and the Self. New York, Basic Books, 1971

13. Albano AM, Chorpita BF: Treatment of anxiety disorders. Psychiatr Clin North Am 18:767–783, 1995

14. Messer SB, Warren CS: Models of Brief Psychodynamic Therapy. New York, Guilford, 1995

15. Dulcan M, Piercy P: A model for teaching and evaluating brief psychotherapy with children and their families. Professional Psychology: Research and Practice 16:689–700, 1985

16. Weisz JR, Donenberg GR, Han S, et al: Bridging the gap between laboratory and clinic in child and adolescent psychotherapy. J Consult Clin Psychol 63:688–701, 1995

17. Smyrnios KX, Kirkby RJ: Long-term comparison of brief versus unlimited psychodynamic treatments with children and their parents. J Consult Clin Psychol 61:1020–1027, 1993

18. Hoagwood K, Hibbs E, Brent D, et al: Introduction to the special section: efficacy and effectiveness in studies of child and adolescent psychotherapy. J Consult Clin Psychol 63:683–687, 1995

19. Yager J, Docherty J, Tischler GL: Training psychiatric residents for managed care. Newsletter of the American Association of Directors of Psychiatric Residency Training, Fall 1996, pp 3–6

9

THE RECIPROCAL RELATIONSHIP BETWEEN PHARMACOTHERAPY AND PSYCHOTHERAPY

> The future may teach us how to exercise a direct influence, by particular chemical substances, upon the amounts of energy and their distribution in the apparatus of the mind. It may be that there are undreamed possibilities of therapy .... (1, p. 182)

Despite Freud's belief in the potential for psychoactive chemicals to aid psychoanalytic work, psychodynamic therapists have been relatively slow in ushering medications into their work. The appearance of this chapter in this book underscores the need for brief dynamic therapists to consider the effective use of medications. In fact, the use of medications during psychotherapy fits quite comfortably within psychoanalytic tradition.

Before embarking on his psychological theories, Freud, about a century ago, was struggling to conceptualize the interrelationship between mind and brain in his Project for a Scientific Psychology (2). As a neurologist, he recognized that brain pathology must have something to do with psychiatric disturbances. However, the limited knowledge of brain function available to him in the latter years of the 19th century sharply limited his theoretical speculations. Now, we are witnessing an explosion of knowledge about the brain. The time is ripe for a renewal of theoretical speculation about the neurology of psychotherapy.

Pharmacotherapy also fits comfortably with the search for meaning within the analytic tradition. Although many analysts had claimed that medication "interfered with the development of the transference," they failed to note the possibility that medications sometimes serve as oval or round blank screens themselves for the projection of myriad idiosyncratic meanings. Purple or red, yellow or green, the little objects serve as variations of Rorschach inkblots that can illuminate patterns of cognitive, emotional, behavioral, and interpersonal dysfunction.

One could hope, then, that a tighter conceptual relationship between mind and brain, between pharmacotherapy and psychotherapy, could lead to more efficient and effective treatments. Research evidence is beginning to accumulate to suggest that combined treatments may be more effective than single treatments alone in the aggregate (3). However, no controlled studies have investigated the potential utility of incorporating the meaning of medications into the psychotherapeutic process or whether and how medications accelerate the psychotherapeutic process. These questions require innovative protocols yet to be developed. Instead, clinicians must rely on astute clinical observation to substantiate and develop the possibility that medications can accelerate the process of psychotherapeutic change, through both their direct pharmacological effects and their idiosyncratic meanings to individual patients.

The first section of this chapter addresses the beginnings of our understanding of the neurology of psychotherapy. It summarizes seminal research in obsessive-compulsive disorder that lays a foundation for solid clinical speculation about the convergent effects of pharmacotherapy and psychotherapy on the "worry circuit." The second section addresses the role medications can play across the stages of psychotherapy. In the third and fourth sections, several examples are offered to illustrate the manner in which reactions to pharmacotherapy reveal key patterns that are useful for psychotherapeutic understanding—a psychodynamics of pharmacotherapy for individuals and families. The next section reemphasizes the value of considering pharmacotherapy as a psychotherapeutic intervention, and the concluding section discusses combined treatment in the era of managed care.

■ OBSESSIVE-COMPULSIVE DISORDER AND THE "WORRY CIRCUIT"

The mind requires the brain in order to function. Therefore, abnormalities in brain function should correlate with abnormal mental functioning. These abnormalities in brain function should disappear with successful mind treatment.

However, we are in the middle of a profound paradigm shift. Most clinicians reflexively consider brain treatments to be medications (or electroconvulsive therapy), whereas psychotherapy is considered a mind treatment. However, psychotherapy treats the mind by altering the brain. Changes in the mind take place through changes in the brain.

This logic now boasts substantive research proof based on positron-emission tomography scans of the living brains of patients with obsessive-compulsive disorder treated with either medication (clomipramine) or behavior therapy (exposure and response prevention). Several areas of the brain appear to be hyperactive (hypermetabolic) in patients with obsessive-compulsive disorder. These areas include the orbital cortex of the frontal lobe and the caudate nucleus of the basal ganglia. Treatment success with either medications or behavior therapy shows close correlations between reductions in the standard measure of obsessive-compulsive disorder (the Yale-Brown Obsessive Compulsive Scale, 4) and reductions in the hypermetabolic activity of the orbital cortex and the caudate nucleus. In other words, both medications and behavior therapy were effective in modulating brain function correlated with a reduction in the symptoms of obsessive-compulsive disorder (5).

The "worry circuit," which may be composed of the thalamus and cingulate gyrus as well as the caudate and orbital cortex (6), could also play a part in other obsessional disorders, including the ruminations of depressed patients and the worries of patients with generalized anxiety disorder. Patients treated with serotonin-selective reuptake inhibitors report that their worries are still present but are not so intense; perhaps the medications reduce the firing rates of the circuit (L. R. Baxter, personal communication, February 1995).

One patient, for example, in the midst of marital turmoil, custody battles with her previous husband, and high anxiety at work, raised her dose of paroxetine (Paxil) from 20 mg to 60 mg. When asked what the medication did, she replied: "It gives me a 'so what.'" Just as cognitive therapists encourage their patients to distance themselves from disturbing thoughts through challenging their beliefs with a "so what," serotonin-selective reuptake inhibitors may help them accomplish the same end. The difference, of course, is that when the medication is withdrawn, the "so what" tends to disappear. On the other hand, can therapists think of medications like this as catalysts to reach states of mind that could be achievable by nonpharmacological means?

■ PSYCHOPHARMACOLOGY DURING THE STAGES OF PSYCHOTHERAPY

The tendency to dichotomize mind and brain, as suggested by René Descartes, has fostered the conceptual separation of pharmacotherapy and psychotherapy. Different clinicians sometimes perform different tasks as dictated by law, one giving pills, the other doing psychotherapy. Psychiatrists, who may perform both pharmacotherapy and psychotherapy, also tend to dichotomize the treatments within the clinical consultation, asking patients, "How are you doing with your medication?" In many instances, this encapsulated discussion serves the purpose of symptom-focused monitoring. There are times, however, when the alert psychotherapist can use the idea that medications may function as another psychotherapeutic intervention. To do so requires that psychotherapy be defined in generic terms rather than psychodynamic, cognitive, behavioral, systems, or existential-humanistic terms.

The common-factors approach to psychotherapy integration offers this possibility (7).

Psychotherapy is based on an interpersonal relationship following a problem-solving sequence that contains stages, each of which has discernible objectives. In the most common dyadic form, the pair must engage in a working alliance, define patterns to change, initiate and maintain change, and then terminate (8). Pharmacotherapy can aid as well as impede the accomplishment of the goals of each of these stages (Table 9–1).

Clinicians generally recognize that medications can aid in the engagement process and, conversely, that sometimes a strong working alliance must be developed in psychotherapy before patients will accept medications (9). Less well accepted are the psychodynamic and systems aspects of pharmacotherapy. The clinician who is willing to consider mind-brain crossings by speculating about the meaning of certain idiosyncratic patient reactions will be rewarded with a quicker, clearer definition of problematic psychological patterns. In addition, medications sometimes act as deviators from current family system equilibria, thereby creating disequilibria that may aid or subvert the therapeutic process. These modest conceptual shifts appear likely to aid in treatment efficiency, although research supporting these claims will be difficult to produce.

■ PHARMACOTHERAPY HIGHLIGHTS KEY DYSFUNCTIONAL PATTERNS

Medication Compliance and a Key Cognitive Pattern

Taking pills has meaning, and so does discontinuing them. Examining the reasoning behind irrational medication discontinuation and its consequences can serve as an illustration of a key dysfunctional pattern, just as any out-of-the-ordinary set of nonpharmacological behaviors can. Consider the following examples.

TABLE 9–1. **Stages of individual psychotherapy: a medication emphasis**

Stage	Engagement	Pattern search	Change	Termination
Goals	Trust Credibility Report self-observations	To define problem patterns that, if changed, would lead to a desirable outcome	Relinquish old pattern(s) Initiate new pattern(s) Practice new pattern(s)	To separate efficiently
Techniques	Convey empathic understanding Effective suggestions Effective medications	Questionnaires Homework Idiosyncratic meanings ascribed to medication	Interpretation Cognitive change Behavioral suggestion Medication-induced change	Mutually agreed Patient initiates Therapist initiates Medication influenced (e.g., side effect)
Content	Medication responsive Diagnosis	Does response to medication reflect a problem pattern?	Medication effects or insight around medication use accelerates change	Medications may prolong termination
Resistance	Are excessive side effects resistant to treatment?	Does pattern of non-adherence to medication regimen reflect a problem pattern?	Do new side effects suggest resistance to change?	Symptom recurrence not necessarily indication for medication change

Transference	For example, physician seen as malevolent or all-powerful	Is key interpersonal pattern reflected in transaction about medication?	Unresolved distortions may be signaled by a new medication issue inhibiting change	Desire for new or more medication reflects desire to hold therapist
Countertransference	For example, physician failure to prescribe appropriately	Medication prescription reflects distorted response to patient	Sudden change in regimen reflects an attempt to undermine change	New medication reflects desire to keep contact

Source. Adapted from Beitman BD: "Medications During Psychotherapy: Case Studies of the Reciprocal Relationship Between Psychotherapy Process and Medication Use," in *Integrating Pharmacotherapy and Psychotherapy.* Edited by Beitman BD, Klerman GL. Washington, DC, American Psychiatric Press, 1991, pp. 21–43.

Case 1

Mr. K, a 37-year-old travel agent, was being successfully treated for panic attacks with imipramine. He felt so normal that on a return trip from Hawaii he decided to discontinue the medication. On the plane, he had another panic attack. He reasoned that his panic attack was probably triggered by his fear of airplanes and his reluctance to return to the chaos of his family home. He seemed to ignore, however, that stopping his imipramine may have also contributed to the attack.

When asked whether he also had major blind spots in other parts of his life, he replied, "Yes, most definitely. My wife repeatedly points out to me the obvious things I miss with the children, and especially her." He was now open to new perspectives.

As-Needed Ingestion Illustrates a Key Interpersonal Pattern

Cognitive and behavior therapists have long emphasized the great value of diaries in targeting symptomatic behavior. Patients can, in this way, use the many hours of the week not spent in therapy to gather data about their own difficulties. Patterns become more quickly recognized. One of the clear oversights of most dynamic therapies is the failure to utilize this simple, effective idea. As-needed ingestion of medications can be considered as an example of dysfunctional behavior, just as panic attacks and increases in depression, smoking, and drinking serve as targets for psychotherapeutic efforts, as illustrated in the following case.

Case 2

Ms. L, a 55-year-old, divorced insurance executive, had been taking butalbital (Fiorinal) for many years, as prescribed by her family physician for headaches. Her psychiatrist asked her to record the times she took the medication. Much to her surprise, she discovered that she often took it shortly after being criticized or frustrated by a colleague or employer. This relationship helped to reduce her butalbital intake and facilitated her examination of this extreme sensitivity to frustration and criticism.

Transference and Countertransference

Like any other psychotherapeutic intervention, the transaction involving medications can involve significant distortions on the part of therapist and patient. Following are some brief descriptions.

Case 3

A 28-year-old male therapist had a 23-year-old female patient who had developed a strong sexualized transference to him. The therapist could not consider himself attractive to women because sexuality disturbed him. He offered the patient a benzodiazepine. He was correct that someone was anxious, but he had selected the wrong person (10).

Other examples:

1. Countertransference: A therapist is unconsciously angry at a patient, prescribes a side effect–prone medication, and tells the patient to come back in 3 months.
2. Transference: A patient makes a suicide attempt with the therapist's medications, implying that "you are killing me."
3. Transference-countertransference: A patient tests the psychiatrist's degree of caring by demanding large doses of potentially addictive medications.
4. Transference: As an indirect expression of anger at the therapist, a patient complains of excessive side effects from a medication previously taken for several months with no side effects.

Benzodiazepine Disinhibition Reveals Dysfunctional Patterns

In a small percentage of patients, benzodiazepines can unleash angry, aggressive, or paranoid states. A subset of these responses can highlight dysfunctional patterns, as illustrated in the following two cases.

Case 4

Ms. M, who was age 30, married, and unhappy and had been diagnosed with borderline personality disorder, took an overdose of alprazolam (Xanax) to forget everything. She was in therapy for 2 years and had begun to develop a strong attachment to her male psychiatrist but had up to this point behaved in a meek, passive, and compliant manner. On the overdose of alprazolam, she became an angry, vindictive, foul-mouthed adolescent. She hated her therapist, and no one could tell her what to do. She wanted what she wanted and was going to get it. A brief hospitalization was required. After another year of therapy, this part of her emerged in the transference, becoming at times psychotic as she demanded the body and soul of her psychiatrist. She was again angry and vindictive when she did not get her way. She could only dimly comprehend the unrealistic nature of her demands. The disinhibition response had revealed the future evolution of the transference.

Case 5

Ms. N, age 44, took a small dose of clonazepam for her panic attacks and felt better. She took a little more and felt even better. A little more, and she was full of energy and needed little sleep. But then she began to suspect that people in school were mistreating her daughter and that perhaps she needed to purchase a gun to protect her. Then she remembered that she supported gun control legislation and began to question her motives. Her psychiatrist suggested that she immediately discontinue taking the clonazepam. Her delusion dissipated. Further inspection of these paranoid thoughts revealed a close connection to her own childhood in which she was abused physically and emotionally by a highly religious set of parents who were part of a culture that tolerated the mistreatment of girls. In protecting her daughter, she was trying to do what no one had done for her as a child. This revelation set the stage for moving away from her mother who lived down the street and finally claiming a life of her own, away from the abusive culture of her parents. The move correlated with a steady diminution of her agoraphobic symptoms.

■ PHARMACOTHERAPY ALTERS MARITAL AND FAMILY DYNAMICS

Marital and family systems function at sometimes fragile equilibria. The introduction of change through medications and psychotherapy can sometimes reverberate through such systems to new states, some of which are desirable and some not. Sometimes one member improves only to reveal dysfunction in another. Some families have much trouble adjusting to normalization of a depressed or anxious member who had been dysfunctional for many years. Some marriages dissolve when the apparently dysfunctional member improves. The following cases illustrate how medications in systems seem to trigger anticipated and sometimes unanticipated changes.

Medication Helps to Save Family Integrity

Occasionally, medications do what people hope they will do: almost magically turn around a deteriorating situation. Rather than facing divorce and custody battles, sometimes families are saved.

Case 6

Ms. O could no longer tolerate her husband's (Mr. P) irritability and agoraphobia. The children could not be around him without being yelled at or criticized. Mr. P could not travel beyond the limits of their small town. He had been agoraphobic before they were married but had never bothered to tell her. Now they had two young children, and she could never go with Mr. P to her family gatherings 60 miles away or on any other small outing. Desperately, she sought help, not for herself but for him, from a psychiatrist in another town, because there was none in their town. Because Mr. P could not travel outside of his town limits, the psychiatrist talked to him on the phone. Mr. P had panic attacks and depression in addition to agoraphobia. With some trepidation, the psychiatrist prescribed imipramine without seeing the patient and emphasized a behavioral approach to his agoraphobia: travel increasingly greater distances from town. Mr. P became less depressed and less irritable while taking the imipramine and, after 2 years of prodding by Ms. O, showed up in the psychiatrist's office 30 miles away. They had gone to the annual family picnic. Ms. O was delighted.

Medications as Markers for Marital Difficulties

Tracking how medications fit into interpersonal transactions may illustrate interpersonal problems, as suggested by the next example.

Case 7

Ms. R, age 26, requested psychotherapy and medication 1 year after having made a serious suicide attempt in which she had taken her husband's antidepressant and lithium. Since her hospitalization, she had been maintaining herself on her husband's medications because her previous therapist had refused to refer her for them. (This use of his medications suggested that she was angry at her husband and that she was also dependent on him because she had used the pills in a suicide attempt and continued to need him to supply them for her afterward.)

Ms. R very much wanted independence from her husband. However, she continued to believe that she needed lithium, although she was not bipolar. Her psychiatrist prescribed lithium in low doses, allowing her to have her own supply. This intervention appeared to provide a deviation in the marital interaction pattern, which became amplified. She became more self-reliant; her husband could not accommodate to her increased independence, and they eventually divorced (11).

Request for Pharmacotherapy for Spouse Helps to Highlight a Marital Pattern

The alert clinician seeks to define single instances of a pattern of potentially dysfunctional behavior. The arena for such behavior includes the relationship between the patient and the therapist and the boundaries of that relationship.

Case 8

Mr. S wanted help with his marriage again. He had seen two previous therapists for the same reason. He had terminated with his second therapist in order for his wife to be seen by him after they had been in brief couples therapy with this therapist. Mr. S acquiesced to his wife in many other ways. She was agoraphobic with panic attacks, so they traveled little, usually stayed on the first floor of hotels, and traveled only by car, stopping frequently. One day he brought home his favorite freshly baked pie—cherry. She ate it all with no complaint from him. After several sessions, Mr. S asked his psychiatrist to see his wife for a medication evaluation, even though she had another psychiatrist. "After all," said Mr. S, "you are the best in town in treating panic disorder." His psychiatrist refused. Mr. S pleaded. "Remember your last therapist. Remember the cherry pie," said the psychiatrist. "You could at least call her," said Mr. S. "No!" said the psychiatrist.

This "no!" seems to have served as a model for Mr. S's increasing ability to not give into his wife's demands and requests. He no longer responded to her every whim. They separated, then divorced. Her agoraphobia became significantly less severe after the divorce. The nonconsultation for pharmacotherapeutic management had helped her to a positive change in her symptoms (9).

■ CATALYSTS FOR CHANGE

The emphasis of managed care on efficient, effective, high-quality treatment is forcing mental health practitioners to dramatically reevaluate what they are doing and how they think about what they are doing. One crucial conceptual shift involves the self-defined role as therapist. Greenson (12) characterized transference interpretation as "the ultimate and decisive instrument" (p. 39), echoing many years of psychoanalytic belief in the therapist's words as scalpels of change. This ringing affirmation of the therapist's power to change patients resembles the belief of many pharmacotherapists (as well as psychopharmacologically naive therapists) that medications change people. In both scenarios, the psychopharmacologist-psychoanalyst, surgeonlike, operates on the passive psyche of the patient.

This interpersonal treatment schema for both medications and interpretations is being altered in the era of managed care. Therapists cannot assume the great burden implied. Patients must be clearly held accountable for instituting changes. And the therapist-psychopharmacologist is becoming a catalyst, an enzyme, for change.

How can this idea, well accepted among psychotherapists, be substantiated for pharmacotherapy? In a recently reported study, patients entering a panic disorder treatment trial with placebo or a new benzodiazepine completed the Stages of Change questionnaire (13). This 32-item scale measured patient readiness to change across a four-category continuum. The study found that readiness to change predicted outcome in both the placebo and active drug groups. Those whose answers reflected a greater readiness to change changed more positively than those who seemed less ready to change. Therefore, medications, like other psychotherapeutic interventions, are incorporated into patients' own commitment to change and are coupled with their other coping strategies to bring about desired change.

This shift in pharmacological and psychotherapeutic views about medications underlies the cases reported in this chapter. Medications are sometimes simply another psychotherapeutic intervention.

■ COMBINED TREATMENT IN THE ERA OF MANAGED CARE

The pressures of cost savings are driving psychiatrists away from the practice of psychotherapy. The old mental health clinic model of the psychotherapy triangle—a pharmacotherapist, a nonmedical psychotherapist, and a patient—appears to be gaining ascendancy under managed care. Older psychiatrists, trained and experienced in long-term psychotherapy, are bitterly confronting a rapidly changing payment system that eliminates them from doing what they have grown to love.

If psychiatrists are to continue to do psychotherapy, the most likely venue will be as dual treaters—using both pharmacotherapy and psychotherapy. The key question for future research is: Under what conditions is it more cost-effective to have one person providing both medications and psychotherapy? Managers, whether physicians themselves or administrators, will want to have answers to this question. Here is a preliminary set of hypotheses.

Patients with severe DSM-IV (14) diagnoses are likely to be more efficiently treated by one person, because the interaction between medications and psychotherapy may be tighter. For example, a patient with moderate major depression may respond quickly and easily to a serotonin-selective reuptake inhibitor; the medication will make her more readily able to use psychotherapy, whether provided by the pharmacotherapist or psychotherapist. On the other hand, a person with bipolar disorder may start feeling good or bad because of a mix of influences—biochemical and environmental. Teasing out the distinction; making modest adjustment in medications; and understanding interactions between pharmacotherapy, endocrine function, and psychosocial influence would be more efficiently accomplished by one person who is knowledgeable in biological as well as psychosocial areas.

Nevertheless, if psychiatrists are to continue practicing psychotherapy, they must learn to do so better. Psychiatrists' time costs more than social workers' time. Therefore, psychiatrists must learn how to be that much more efficient at providing therapy as they are paid relative to nonmedical practitioners.

Finally, in pharmacologically stabilized patients, a medication check takes perhaps 5 minutes, including rewriting the prescription. If the time allotted is 20–30 minutes, there could be adequate time for brief therapy.

The practice of medicine is being severely challenged by revolutionary changes in the system by which physicians are paid. Psychiatry's identity as a profession lies on the interface between mind and brain. Our practice straddles and integrates the concepts of psyche and soma. Combining pharmacotherapy and psychotherapy lies at the heart of clinical psychiatry.

■ REFERENCES

1. Freud S: An outline of psychoanalysis (1940), in The Standard Edition of the Complete Psychological Works of Sigmund Freud, Vol 23. Translated and edited by Strachey J. London, Hogarth Press, pp 141–208

2. Freud S: Project for a scientific psychology (1895), in The Standard Edition of the Complete Psychological Works of Sigmund Freud, Vol 1. Translated and edited by Strachey J. London, Hogarth Press, 1966, pp 281–397

3. Sperry L: Psychopharmacology and Psychotherapy. New York, Brunner/Mazcl, 1995

4. Goodman WK, Price LH, Rassmussen SA, et al: The Yale-Brown Obsessive-Compulsive Scale, II: validity. Arch Gen Psychiatry 46:1012–1016, 1989

5. Schwartz JM: Cognitive-behavioral self-treatment for obsessive-compulsive disorder systematically alters cerebral metabolism: a mind-brain interaction paradigm for psychotherapists, in Obsessive-Compulsive Disorder: Diagnosis, Etiology, Treatment. Edited by Hollander E, Stein DJ. New York, Marcel Dekker, 1994, pp 88–122

6. Baxter LR: Neuroimaging studies of human anxiety disorders: cutting paths of knowledge through the field of neurotic phenomena, in Psychopharmacology: The Fourth Generation of Progress. Edited by Bloom FE, Kupfer DJ. New York, Raven, 1995, pp 66–101

7. Norcross JC, Goldfried MR: Handbook of Psychotherapy Integration. New York, Basic Books, 1992

8. Beitman BD: The Structure of Individual Psychotherapy. New York, Guilford, 1987

9. Beitman BD: Medications during psychotherapy: case studies of the reciprocal relationship between psychotherapy process and medication use, in Integrating Pharmacotherapy and Psychotherapy. Edited by Beitman BD, Klerman GL. Washington, DC, American Psychiatric Press, 1991, pp 21–43

10. Langs R: Psychoanalytic Psychotherapy. Northvale, NJ, Jason Aronson, 1973

11. Beitman BD: Combining pharmacotherapy and psychotherapy: process considerations, in Psychobiology and Psychopharmacology—2. Edited by Flach F. New York, WW Norton, 1988, pp 71–92

12. Greenson RR: The Technique and Practice of Psychoanalysis, Vol 1. New York, International Universities Press, 1967

13. Beitman BD, Beck NC, Deuser WE, et al: Patient stage of change predicts outcome in a panic disorder medication trial. Anxiety 1:64–69, 1994

14. American Psychiatric Association: Diagnostic and Statistical Manual of Mental Disorders, 4th Edition. Washington, DC, American Psychiatric Association, 1994

INDEX

Page numbers printed in **boldface** *type refer to tables or figures.*